GROWING OUR FUTURE

Kumarian Press Library of Management for Development
Selected Titles

Promises Not Kept: The Betrayal of Social Change in the Third World, John Isbister

Gender Analysis in Development Planning: A Case Book, edited by Aruna Rao, Mary B. Anderson, and Catherine Overholt

Breaking the Cycle of Poverty: The BRAC Strategy, Catherine Lovell

Managing Quality of Care in Population Programs, edited by Anrudh K. Jain

Democratizing Development: The Role of Voluntary Organizations, John Clark

Opening the Marketplace to Small Enterprise: Where Magic Ends and Development Begins, Ton de Wilde and Stijntje Schreurs, with Arleen Richman

Working Together: Gender Analysis in Agriculture, Vols. 1 and 2, edited by Hilary Sims Feldstein and Susan V. Poats

Getting to the 21st Century: Voluntary Action and the Global Agenda, David C. Korten

Toward a Green Central America: Integrating Conservation and Development, edited by Valerie Barzetti and Yanina Rovinski

Change in an African Village: Kefa Speaks, Else Skjønsberg

Local Institutional Development: An Analytical Sourcebook with Cases, Norman T. Uphoff

The Water Sellers: A Cooperative Venture by the Rural Poor, Geoffrey D. Wood and Richard Palmer-Jones, with M.A.S. Mandal, Q.F. Ahmed, and S.C. Dutta

Improving Family Planning Evaluation: A Step-by-Step Guide for Managers and Evaluators, José García-Núñez

Gender Roles in Development Projects: A Case Book, edited by Catherine Overholt, Mary B. Anderson, Kathleen Cloud, and James E. Austin

GROWING OUR FUTURE
Food Security and the Environment

editors
Katie Smith
Tetsunao Yamamori

KUMARIAN PRESS

Growing Our Future: Food Security and the Environment

Published 1992 in the United States of America by Kumarian Press, Inc., 630 Oakwood Avenue, Suite 119, West Hartford, Connecticut 06110-1529 USA.

Cover design by Laura Augustine
Book design by Lisa Leff and Jenna Dixon
Copyedited and proofread by Jolene Robinson
Typeset by Lisa Leff
Index prepared by Alan M. Greenberg

Printed in the United States of America by McNaughton and Gunn.
Text printed with soy-based ink on recycled acid-free paper.

Library of Congress Cataloging-in-Publication Data

Growing our future : food security and the environment / editors, Katie Smith, Tetsunao Yamamori.
        p.   cm. — (Kumarian Press library of management for development)
    Based on papers presented at a conference held November 1991 at Arizona State University.
    Includes bibliographical references and index.
    ISBN 1-56549-014-2 (pbk. : alk. paper)
    1. Food supply—Congresses. 2. Sustainable agriculture—Congresses. I. Smith, Katie, 1960–   . II. Yamamori, Tetsunao, 1937–   . III. Series.
HD9000.5.G78   1992
338.1'9—dc20   92-9645

---

96   95   94   93   92   5   4   3   2   1
First Printing 1992

CONTENTS

FOREWORD

IN NOVEMBER 1991, FOOD FOR the Hungry and Arizona State University (ASU) hosted a landmark meeting between conservation and development interests. The conference was in preparation for the June 1992 United Nations Conference on Environment and Development (UNCED), or "Earth Summit," but its effect as a motor in a citizens movement for sustainable development will carry far beyond.

The meeting was notable in bringing church-based and nonchurch-based groups together to discuss the ethics of development and environmental degradation. Over 100 participants, representing five continents and a number of professions, united in their judgment that civilizations crumble when individuals indulge in self-interest more than the interests of the total population.

The Earth is out of whack. In his opening remarks, keynote speaker Calvin B. DeWitt of the University of Wisconsin said, "We must first seek the wholeness and integrity of Creation, not self-interest; seeking Creation's integrity first brings sustainable (resource) wealth...Integrity of Creation is the necessary prerequisite for achieving food security; without this, food insecurity will be chronic." This presentation set the scene for some leading minds from conservation and development sectors to put forward people-centered ideals, values, and resolutions aimed at achieving such integrity.

In addition, as the papers and resolutions presented here propose, we world citizens must ask ourselves, "Will I conduct myself in a way that is self-centered, God-centered, or other-centered?" We must each consider what is needed to help bring the Earth back into balance.

There is no one answer. Instead, the answer lies in melding con–servation and development issues into a cohesive, people-to-people, farm-to-farm, community-to-community campaign. The answer abides within each of us.

Food for the Hungry and ASU are to be commended for making this symposium happen, and for helping to inform the United Nations and world governments of what needs to be done to avoid the collapse of our civilization due to too many people basking for too long in self-interests that threaten to destroy the core of our existence: our environment.

The Honorable Tony P. Hall, Chair
Select Committee on Hunger
House of Representatives
United States of America

PREFACE

Tetsunao Yamamori

Tetsunao Yamamori, president of Food for the Hungry, is an adjunct professor of sociology at Arizona State University whose first brush with hunger came as a child in Japan during World War II. He holds a doctorate from Duke University and has authored more than a dozen books and articles on church-based development work.

FOOD FOR THE HUNGRY WAS privileged to host a symposium, Growing Our Future: Food Security and the Environment, in November, 1991 with the Arizona State University (ASU) School of Agribusiness and Environmental Resources. The meeting was a grassroots effort by individuals and organizations to take action on behalf of the world. It was a strong current in a rising tide of citizens' voices calling for sustainable development. Participants suggested policy steps to be presented at the 1992 United Nations Conference on Environment and Development (UNCED), in Rio de Janeiro, Brazil. The process involved attempts to clarify the issues at stake and actions needed in at least one crucial and timeless realm—that of poverty and environmental degradation, where hungry people's need for sustainable agriculture and the land's need for wise conservation meet.

Participants came from across the nation and around the world, from government, conservation, and international development sectors, business, academia, and churches. This unique cross section of people learned from each other as they experienced a piece of the Rio process in Tempe, Arizona.

Those of us working to prevent hunger and protect the environment must occasionally examine our motivations. Mine springs from a near-starvation experience as a child in Japan at the end of World War II. Since then, I have been committed to ending the atrocity of hunger. I became keenly aware of the importance of protecting the environment to safeguard the food supply during Food for the Hungry's involvement in emergency feeding during the 1984 Ethiopian famine and subsequent rural rehabilitation work. In 1985, the hills of the region in which we worked were barren, completely deforested. The topsoil was gone. Great gullies of erosion carved the hillsides. In Ethiopia, strengthening food security meant helping people to plant trees, terrace, and build check dams. Today, five years later, those same hillsides are covered with young forests, wild animals have returned, and the soil is producing. This year, when drought again hit the country and this region, the areas where we had helped local people to conserve soil and plant trees were in food surplus.

The United Nations recently reported that 930 million people in developing countries subsist in survival mode, never sure where to find their next meal, understandably choosing short-term gains over the environmental impact of their desperate attempts to feed themselves and their families. Destructive farming practices of the poor on the one hand, and overindustralization, overconsumption, effects of war, drought and trade, on the other, join to create increasingly unproductive cropland.

Food for the Hungry is pleased to provide these proceedings to those interested in bringing the Earth back into balance. They embody what each symposium participant has learned through struggles with the issue, and contain specific recommendations to policymakers in Rio, our nations, and our communities.

Acknowledgments

Many groups met across the nation and around the world in 1991 to do their homework for UNCED. Growing Our Future was a collaborative, international non-governmental organization (NGO) effort, with financial support coming from several organizations, primarily Japan International Food for the Hungry (Dr. Eisuke Kanda, Executive Director), our Japanese partner NGO. Many thanks to Eric Thor, Dean of the Arizona State University School of Agribusiness and Environmental Resources, for cosponsoring the symposium, and to InterAction, World Wildlife Fund, Audubon, World Neighbors, World Vision, and the U.S. Citizens Network on UNCED, for their cooperation in organizing and publicizing the conference and their financial support of conference speakers.

The following people gave their time, talent, and knowledge to make the meeting meaningful.

Speakers and Facilators
Gloria Barbier-Lara, TechnoServe
Antonio Calzada-Rovirosa, Arizona State University
Jason Clay, Cultural Survival, Boston
Calvin DeWitt (keynote), University of Wisconsin/Au Sable Institute
Milton Flores, Director of International Covercrop Clearinghouse
    of Honduras
Timothy R. Frankenberger, University of Arizona
Richard Gordon, Arizona State University
Anne Keeney, InterAction
Hershey Leaman, Mennonite Central Committee
Atherton E. Martin, The Development Institute, Dominica
Sharon Schoenhals, Food for the Hungry
Dan Shaffer, School of Agribusiness and Environmental Resources,
    Arizona State University
Robin Shell, Food for the Hungry
Katie Smith, Food for the Hungry
Frances Spivy-Weber, U.S. Citizens Network on UNCED and the
    National Audubon Society
Eric Thor, Dean, School of Agribusiness and Environmental
    Resources, Arizona State University
Jack Hood Vaughn, USAID's Regional Office on Central America
    in Guatemala City

Case Study Presenters
Jason Clay, Cultural Survival
Frank G. Cookingham, World Vision
Calvin DeWitt, Au Sable Institute/University of Wisconsin
Randy Hoag, Food for the Hungry
Andreas Lehnoff, Defensores de la Naturaleza
Eric Thor, Arizona State University

Case Study Facilitators
Bradley L. Ack, World Wildlife Fund
Neilson C. Conklin, Arizona State University
Timothy R. Frankenberger, University of Arizona
Robin Shell, Food for the Hungry
Paul Thompson, World Vision
Tom Zopf, Food Aid Management/CARE

Panelists
Bradley L. Ack, World Wildlife Fund

Ginny Hildebrand, Association of Arizona Food Banks
Charles Owubah, Purdue University
Joe Quiroz, The Nature Conservancy

The following persons organized and documented the event.

Organizers
Lori Baer, School of Agribusiness and Environmental Resources,
    Arizona State University
Dee Delvechio, College of Agriculture and Environmental Design,
    Arizona State University
Denise Rupert, Food for the Hungry
Katie Smith, Food for the Hungry, Symposium Director
Fritz Steiner, College of Agriculture and Environmental Design,
    Arizona State University
Eric Thor, School of Agribusiness and Environmental Resources,
    Arizona State University
Kristin Wedan, Food for the Hungry
Bob Wheeler, Food for the Hungry
Charles Babbitt, Maricopa Audubon Society

Artist
Lisa Leff, Food for the Hungry

Rapporteurs
Scott Allen, Food for the Hungry
Marcia Barkis, American Graduate School of International Management
Carolyn Crusel, American Graduate School of International Management
Jackie Gomez, Arizona State University
Don Graham, Food for the Hungry, Proceedings Editor
Pam Mischen, Arizona State University
Miles Smith, American Graduate School of International Management
Maureen Ward, Arizona State University

Publicity Coordinator
Karen Randau, Food for the Hungry

Proceedings Readers/Editors
Ted Okada, Food for the Hungry
Karen Randau, Food for the Hungry
Carole Hertzler, Food for the Hungry

INTRODUCTION

Katie Smith

Katie Smith, a former journalist with The Wall Street Journal *and* Montreal Gazette *and researcher at Harvard's Kennedy School of Government, is international program coordinator for Food for the Hungry. She is a graduate of Stanford University and the Free University of Brussels with seven years of experience in African, Latin American, and North American Native issues.*

POVERTY AND LAND DEGRADATION ARE two sides of the same worn coin. We know it, we talk about it, but fora are few where development and conservation practitioners can compare notes and combine forces to overcome the problem. *Growing Our Future* chronicles an exciting and crucial exchange of ideas between sectors that climaxed with spokespersons for conservation, international development, church missions, government, and industry agreeing on a starting point for uprooting hunger and keeping the Earth: people-centered development.

The symposium, held at Arizona State University in November 1991, preceded the United Nations Conference on Environment and Development (or Earth Summit) June 1992 in Rio de Janeiro, and drew more than 100 conservationists, agriculturalists and resource managers from Africa, Asia, Europe, Latin America and North America. Moreover, "Growing Our Future" was just one current in a rising tide of citizen powered initiatives for sustainable development, a tide that should carry us far beyond Rio to a healthier planet. "Think globally, act locally," said symposium contributor Frances Spivy-Weber, of the National Audubon Society. And when thinking locally, forget not global implications. Said another contributor, Atherton Martin, of The

1

Development Institute of Dominica, "People are the essential ingredient in food security...and the environment." The magic is not in the marketplace, he adds, it's in those who go to the market.

So what does that mean for the average citizen? First, that we mustn't confuse development, or enterprise, with growth. Healthy human development necessitates the right kind of growth, at the right time, in the right way. Growth, unchecked, equals cancer. This is true for our country, our state, our cities, our communities. Calvin DeWitt, an environmental scientist from the University of Wisconsin, brings home this point in *Ethics, Ecosystems and Enterprise: Discovering the Meaning of Food Security and Development.* "It may be a compliment to tell your six-year-old niece on her birthday that you hope she grows four inches in the next year," he told the symposium, "but it's usually not a compliment to tell her mother that you hope she gains forty pounds." Likewise, it is not always a compliment to a small country to say "I hope your gross national product (the total value of all goods and services) doubles next year," or to a small community, "I hope your industry or population triples." DeWitt asserts that our built-in sense that growth that degrades nature is wrong attests to our equally innate sense of the integrity of Creation. He cites a convergence of environmental concern in the world's major religions, and draws on Judeo-Christian tradition to develop three ethical principles for enterprise that derive from ecosystem principles of life.

Second, we need to focus on causes of hunger and environmental degradation, not just symptoms. Our forests are disappearing at a rate of 100,000 square kilometers a year, accelerating plant and animal extinctions to three species per day. Water quality is deteriorating rapidly, we're losing topsoil for farming, and filling the air we breathe with pollutants. Yet these, for the most part, are symptoms of the problem: the root causes are poverty on the one hand, and overconsumption on the other. In *People-Centered Development, Democracy and the Environment,* Atherton E. Martin puts forward an alternative for sustainable development whereby people are at the center of efforts to transform dependent agricultural economies into more self-reliant, ecologically sound systems. He paints a continuum on which change first begins locally, then spreads regionally and nationally, in order to effectively set priorities for actions that will cut consumption in the North and alleviate poverty in the South. In *Resource Wars: Nation-State Conflicts of the 20th Century,* Jason W. Clay of Cultural Survival warns us to consider, in any intervention to promote food security in the North or South, whose land and whose markets are being cultivated. "I don't know of one square acre of land in the world unclaimed by some people group," says Clay. He stresses that the question of resource ownership between states (modern governments) and nations (indigenous people groups sharing a common culture, language, history and territorial base) will become increasingly salient in people-centered development in the nineties. Indeed, events in Eastern Europe, Central Asia and the Horn of Africa are bearing this out. Clay says that giving nations greater ownership of their environment via political autonomy, land rights, and language protection will go a long way toward reversing a root cause of environmental degradation.

Jack Hood Vaughn, environmental counsellor for the United States Agency for International Development, stresses in *Food Security, Environment and Agrarian Reform: Failures and Opportunities in Latin America* the importance of getting development messages to the farms through effective agricultural extension, and getting citizen messages to governments. Write your national representative, call your mayor, and above all, show by doing: volunteer. "Volunteers basically are the ones who win campaigns—military, political and other," says Vaughn. "(They) keep us honest and productive."

They are also a key measure of the appropriateness of a development intervention. For example, Milton Flores, of the International Covercrop Clearinghouse in Honduras, judges the worth of agricultural extension efforts by a peasant's willingness to volunteer to teach his or her neighbors new farming methods. In Flores' paper, *The Human Farm: People-Based Approach to Food Production and Conservation*, coauthored with Elías Sánchez, the new techniques themselves become merely a tool for increasing peasants' environmental understanding. "If the mind of a campesino is a desert, his farm will look like a desert," quotes Flores.

Timothy R. Frankenberger and Daniel M. Goldstein, both of the University of Arizona, encourage nongovernmental organizations (NGOs) to work at the grassroots in Africa to strengthen local community support networks and buffer household food security. This would deter peasants from degrading their environment to cope with hunger in the short term. Frankenberger and Goldstein instruct NGOs to link short-term food security to long-term environmental concerns in the design of interventions, and give frameworks for doing so. Meanwhile, Richard S. Gordon and Antonio Calzada-Rovirosa, both of Arizona State University, have a private sector approach. They link strengthening food security and environmental conservation to ownership. They advocate a current and controversial privatization of both agricultural extension work and land *(ejidos)* in Mexico, and the

establishment of agribusiness "incubators," where fledgling enterprises can hatch together sharing basic services under one roof.

In *Food, Family, God and Earth: Compete for the Whole*, Frances Spivy-
Weber of the National Audubon Society, who is also national
chairperson of the US Citizens Network on UNCED, draws a lesson
from the Navajo, who chart development in terms of a circle that
includes family, environment, economics and spiritual life. Regardless
of the primary focus, be it industry, church missions, or business, we
need to resist a temptation toward tunnel vision and instead view
organizational goals within a broad context of sustainable development. "Compete for the whole," says Fran, "not just a part."

Growing Our Future concludes with six case studies (Appendix I)
showing a range of project responses to the practical challenges of
designing NGO programs that alleviate hunger and poverty while
preserving the Earth's ecological equilibrium. Participants divided into
small groups to discuss these cases Day 2 of the symposium, and put
practical flesh on the theoretical bones of Day 1's paper presentations.
The first three cases are grassroots responses, including descriptions
and lessons learned from World Vision's Tuareg Rehabilitation Project
in Mali; a tropical forest conservation project in Sierra de las Minas,
Guatemala, supported by World Wildlife Fund and Defensores de la
Naturaleza; and a high-altitude greenhouse project in Bolivia's altiplano launched by Food for the Hungry. The remaining three cases are
institutional responses, including a look at church missions' historic
and often negative impact on environmental conservation, with suggestions for redressment in *Missionary Earthkeeping* from Au Sable
Institute; a look at state and local government's use of food aid as a
weapon during drought and war in the Horn of Africa in 1985, in *Food
and Famine in Ethiopia: Weapons Against Cultural Diversity*, from Cultural Survival; and the ASU Center for Agribusiness Policy Studies'
analysis of the Uruguay Round stalemate over agricultural subsidies
in the General Agreement on Tariffs and Trade, in *Getting to GATT*.

The case study groups evolved into policy resolution groups that,
based on symposium discussions, hammered out mandates for
policymakers headed to Rio. These are included in Appendix II.
Many of these resolutions, which were carried to a second phase of
NGO consultation on UNCED in Paris in December 1991, have become part of a global citizens' draft agenda for government action into
the twenty-first century (Agenda 21). The agenda aims to set guidelines for governments to restore and renew the land and our
stewardship of it. Indeed, citizens groups have spoken: we want
healthy lives on a healthy planet. The task at hand is to carry this call

for people-centered, sustainable development to many corners of our communities, our nations, our globe; to identify specific actions needed to advance our goal; and to set an example, each of us in our own backyards, to sow and grow our future.

We the editors and authors offer these proceedings as seeds of thought for the venture.

CHAPTER ONE

ETHICS, ECOSYSTEMS AND ENTERPRISE
Discovering the Meaning of Food Security and Development

Calvin B. DeWitt

Cal DeWitt, a professor of environmental studies from the University of Wisconsin, opened the Symposium with a call to true symbiosis in development and conservation efforts. His views on the ethics of such are rooted in his observations as a wetlands ecologist, in his deep personal faith in the integrity of Creation, and in concrete experience in his own township of Dunn, Wisconsin. There he helped preserve the community's 34.5 square miles of wetlands, woods, and prime agricultural lands through a model stewardship program that turned farmers and weekend fly fisherman alike into environmental watchdogs. DeWitt's notes at the end of the chapter provide Scripture references for his ethical principles, which will be especially interesting to church-based nongovernmental organizations.

AN UNPRECEDENTED AMOUNT OF PUBLISHED information is available today on how the world works. Through highly disciplined research institutions, society has attained substantial understanding of the biosphere and processes that sustain life and its diversity. Laboratories and observatories have yielded comprehensive knowledge of Earth's energy exchange with the sun and outer space, of vital processes of energy flow and material cycling in ecosystems, of fundamental requirements of living things, and of our absolute dependence on all of these. Moreover, agricultural colleges and experiment stations have produced unprecedented technical and practical literature on conservation and stewardship of soils and land. Yet—and this is one of the most astonishing realizations of our time—never in human history have we experienced so great a degradation and destruction of life and environment.

Degradations of Creation[1]

We recently have found that human enterprise alters reception of energy from the sun, with serious consequences for Earth's temperatures and the exposure of life to damaging ultraviolet radiation. Cropland is seriously eroding, being desertified, salinized, and consumed by expanding cities. Primary forests—some 100,000 square kilometers per year—are being removed, accelerating plant and animal extinctions to well over three per day. Water quality—while visibly improved for some surface waters—increasingly deteriorates elsewhere, particularly for groundwater. Biocides made to destroy unwanted plants and animals are carried by global circulations, troubling life near and far. People and cultures are degraded, and impoverishment denies people stewardship of family, community and land; this is accelerated by loss of food varieties and orally transmitted knowledge as traditional cultures and their habitats are consumed by aggressive population expansion.[2]

Ours is not the first decade of recognizing Creation's degradation. In the 1970s, as we all know, tremendous awareness erupted, generating significant response. Legislation was written and adopted; environmentally protective and redemptive technology was invented and installed. Much of the world then rested assured that "the environmental crisis" had been addressed. But near the end of the 1980s we found many problems still with us, as well as many new ones. This is bringing us to an astonishing realization: never has there been greater degradation of Creation than we are experiencing in our time.

Insufficiency of Law and Technique

What is to be made of this apparent failure to address environmental problems adequately? This we have begun to discuss, knowing we have already mobilized technical and legal strategies to unprecedented levels. Through this we are gaining new awareness: we are realizing that technical and legal approaches, while vitally necessary, are not sufficient; techniques might not be adequately deployed and laws not adequately enforced. Moreover, much degradation we find not to be addressable by technique and law alone.

If legal and technical approaches to environmental problems are not sufficient, what is lacking? While initially uncertain of the answer, we have indicators: increasing numbers of environmental scientists—

discontent with mere description of scientific findings—condemn Creation's destruction; philosophers labor to develop environmental ethics; people explore religious traditions for environmental teachings and develop interest in "environmental spirituality"; others invent new religions based on the Gaia hypothesis and other concepts; and institutions such as the International Joint Commission on the Great Lakes write ecosystem ethics while university civil engineering departments introduce ethics into their curricula.[3]

Beyond these indicators, the major world religions are exploring their own traditions for environmental teachings and making environmental ethical pronouncements. Illustrative of these are the Assisi Declarations that announce: that "destruction of the environment and the life depending upon it is a result of ignorance, greed and disregard for the richness of all living things" (Buddhist); we "repudiate all ill-considered exploitation of nature which threatens to destroy it" (Christian); "let us declare our determination to halt the present slide towards destruction, to rediscover the ancient tradition of reverence for all life" (Hindu); God's trustees "are responsible for maintaining the unity of His Creation, the integrity of the Earth, its flora and fauna, its wildlife and natural environment" (Muslim); and "now, when the whole world is in peril, when the environment is in danger of being poisoned and various species, both plant and animal, are becoming extinct, it is our...responsibility to put the defence of nature at the very center of our concern" (Jewish).[4]

A Pursuit of Ethics

All of these indicators point to a searching for a way to live rightly. Each shows the pursuit of ethics—of the question, "What is right?" or "What ought to be?" As we interact with the ecosystems of which we are part and realize the limitations of law and technique, we perceive the need for appropriate ethics. But it is not *mere* ethics. Ethics operate among thieves as well as saints, within organized crime as well as in humanitarian institutions. At its base, an ethical system is a perception of how the world works—a world view by which sense is made of everything. Clearly, in our time, ethics should include a basic understanding of the systems that sustain land and life.

But what is it that we do know? This is a question to which all are open, for whatever our world view, we want it to correspond with reality. Our unprecedented scientific knowledge suggests we have greater potential for a world view consistent with the way the world works than ever before.

Ecosystem Principles

So we ask the bold and necessary question, "How does the world work?" While it may be difficult and even impossible to give a complete answer, we are helped by the integrative concept of "ecosystem" —one that describes the inhabited world. An ecosystem is a set of organisms and components of their physical environment which, through interactions, have developed structural and functional persistence and integrity. Thus, the biosphere—the outer living shell of Earth—is an ecosystem. So too are its constituent parts: forest, lake, prairie, desert, and rotting log.

As ethics addresses "What is right?" the concept of "ecosystem" helps address "How does the world work?" These two strongly interrelate. Understanding ecosystems helps immensely with our present concern. We will next describe and label some of the principles by which they operate. Here are the key ones.

1. *Reciprocity*—each organism—by its production or consumption of oxygen, for example—actively contributes to the life, maintenance, sustenance, and homeostasy of the whole ecosystem.

2. *Continuity*—all present biotic species are the descendants of a very long line of inheritance comprised of those who have survived and flourished in the past. The line of future inheritance—each future organism—is utterly dependent upon these present species. Descendants that overexploit or poorly use resources, or whose line is broken by degradation of habitat, will not produce descendants and their line will be extinguished.

3. *Recovery*—ecosystems and their organisms engage in self-reproduction, rejuvenation, regeneration, and restoration.

4. *Homeostasy*—ecosystems, and the organisms of which they are constituted, employ self-control and self-regulation for maintaining their integrity, at maturity and throughout their development, despite perturbations from a changing environment, within limits.

5. *Community*—in mostly inexplicable ways, ecosystems and their organisms behave and function in ways that, over time, put the survival of kin and ecosystem at a higher priority than individual survival.

6. *Frugality*—organisms take only what is needed to sustain themselves, living within the carrying capacity of the ecosystem, with "luxury consumption" only when surplus is available.[5]
7. *Integrity*—ecosystems are highly ordered systems with wholeness and integrity maintained by self-regulation. Mutually supportive operation between species persists. "Harmful disoperation between species eliminates itself."[6]

This summary will help in basing an environmental ethical system upon knowledge of how the world works. A more adequate approach would be to ground ourselves fully in the ecological literature of natural science.[7] We should note, in passing, that people can override these principles in the short run because of peculiarities of our species, such as our use of money. But for now, this will suffice, together with the following rather poetic summary:

The world works as a symphony of material and life cycles, all powered by Earth's star, the sun, in which solar heating drives the global circulations of water and air in patterns shaped by unequal heating and topographic relief, and solar light energizes through photosynthesis, all of life through a meshwork of molecule-to-molecule and organism-to-organism energy transfers, and in which biotic and physical components, thus empowered, interactively exchange matter and energy to form and maintain the life sustaining biophysical fabric of the biosphere and its component ecosystems.

Ethical Principles

If these ecosystem principles and summary are incorporated into our world view, what are their consequences for an ethical system? Here they are as I see them:[8]

1. *Reflection*—as we are kept through the provisions of land, air, energy flows, and water, so must we keep the Earth.[9] People and others do not merely occupy an ecosystem, but are integral parts who contribute to the benefit from its nurture. People must mirror this nurture in their care for Creation.
2. *Leadership*—we must follow those people who work to prevent and reverse the work of Creation's destroyers, who work to preserve and restore Creation's integrity.[10] People relate differently to Creation: some vandalize it by intent or degrade it by making and accumulating things—careless of breaking the

lineages of biotic species; a few people are benign; and some preserve, restore, and nurture ecosystems of which they are part. It is the last of these types that promote ecosystem and species continuity; it is these that we should emulate.

3. *Fruitfulness*—we may enjoy the fruits of Creation but not degrade or destroy its self-reproducing or self-sustaining fruitfulness.[11] While acceptable to gain sustenance from the Creation's fruits, it is wrong to destroy its ability to be fruitful—to destroy its ability to reproduce plants and animals after their kinds, and its restorative and self-sustaining capacity. Overexploitation or disregard for the household of life is wrong; so is human fruitfulness pursued at the expense of other creatures.

4. *Restoration*—we must not press Creation relentlessly, but allow for its self-sustaining, self-controlling, and developmental functions to operate fully.[12] Providing rest for ourselves and other creatures permits continuation of ecosystem homeostasy—its self-sustaining means to achieve its development and maintain integrity. Providing rest liberates the restorative and regenerative provisions of Creation to make all things new.[13]

5. *Precedence*—we must seek first the wholeness and integrity of Creation, not self-interest.[14] Whatever is gained for self should come as a result of caring for and keeping the Creation—of diligent working to preserve and restore Creation's integrity. Pursuit of material things as first priority will impoverish Creation, reducing Creation's wealth, making us poorer. Seeking Creation's integrity first brings sustainable wealth.

6. *Contentment*—we must seek to maximize contentment, not material gains, and be able to discern the difference.[15] It is not right to have so little food and clothing that we are in jeopardy; thus we should work for these basic needs, moving us toward contentment. But as we move along the spectrum from nothing to more and more, we must not pass the point of contentment or we will degrade human beings, others, and all Creation. All we have is procured from Creation, seeking more than what provides contentment, degrades Creation; an important measure of true wealth is the richness of Creation itself.[16]

7. *Action*—we must not fail to act on what we know is right.[17] There must be integrity—wholeness and oneness—between our knowledge and our actions. Knowledge of the right does no good unless put into practice. Knowledge of ecosystem science, conservation, and stewardship is meaningless if it is merely accumulated and not acted out. The test of human quality is not

in our knowing; it is in what we do with what we know. It is the degree to which we use knowledge for perpetuation and restoration of Creation's integrity.

This summary, together with the previous summary of ecosystem principles, will help in our understanding and conduct of enterprise. We will get there through two summarizing quotations, the first from Aldo Leopold's classic essay, "A Land Ethic,"[18] and the second from a meeting of scientists, theologians and Fourth World people:[19]

"A thing is right when it tends to preserve the integrity, stability, and beauty of the biotic community. It is wrong when it tends otherwise."

"What is just, what is right, is that which maintains the integrity of the ecosystem—that which maintains the social, biological and physical components and their inter-relationships. Development that degrades any of these components or their inter-relationships fosters injustice. True, injustice done by people to people degrades the ecosystem; injustice done by people to plants or animals also degrades the ecosystem. In any such degradation the whole, and eventually every part, suffers."

Thus far we have (1) summarized degradation of Creation, (2) considered the insufficiency of legal and technical responses to this degradation, (3) pointed to the need for ethics to address this insufficiency, (4) identified ecosystems principles, and (5) sketched an ethical framework respectfully supporting these principles. Our task now is to find connections between these principles of ecosystems, ethics, and enterprise, as we work to address the challenges of our time.

Ethics, Ecosystems, and Enterprise

The Prevalence of Impoverishment. At the start, we summarized the many and prevalent degradations of Earth's ecosystems, its creatures and its people. It is now crucial to recognize these degradations for what they are: the impoverishment of Creation—of land, nature, and people. People and others are unable to obtain the means to maintain life and habitat. They are compelled to live at the margins of land and life. This impoverishment is exacerbated by degradation of intrinsic ability of Creation—its ecosystems and its people—to sustain and restore itself. It reduces Creation as provider. Degradation may even extend to impoverishment of the human spirit, to diminution of human dignity, respect, and integrity. This has been poignantly expressed by Russian physicist Irena Erevlua in reference to the explosion of the Chernobyl Power Station: "Planet Earth is very small. It is important to protect it from Chernobyl. Chernobyl produces daily destruction; it is eroding our souls. It is most terrible for our culture."[20]

Impoverishment reaches still further. It is impoverishing Creation as teacher. Creation in its self-sustaining integrity and people in their habitats have always been our most effective teachers. From the "university of nature" we have learned all that we know about the world. The full force of Creation as teacher and its modern erosion I found painfully illustrated en route from Moscow to Leningrad/St. Petersburg, August 15 through September 6, 1991. The Volga ecosystem on whose river we sailed—now "developed" with dams, locks, and ship canals—is disastrously impoverished. The fisheries of its waters and the fruit trees of its hills are gone. Steeples of flooded churches pierce surface waters like candles in the night, their former congregants overwhelmingly diminished. Russian physicist Irena Erevlua, in a lecture given on this journey, sorrowfully observed: "The Volga once fed Russia. It had an abundance of good fish. Springs flowed into the river. There were trout and sturgeon. The Volga River was itself a teacher of the people; it taught them about water, about enterprise, and about spirit. It taught them the habit of communal acting, it made the people think of themselves as members of community. The Volga once fed Russia's soul and spirit. We have lost our teacher!"[21]

Cause of Impoverishment. What is the cause of Creation's impoverishment? Reluctantly, we admit that whatever the sum of modern enterprise—economic, governmental, juridical, charitable, ecclesiastical, educational—and despite benefits given, its net product (obscurely called "by-product") includes rampant environmental degradation, overwhelming expansion of cities and urban poverty, increased hunger, and alienation from Creation as teacher. This is, albeit largely unintended, a product of human actions—a product largely of organized, goal-directed enterprise. Much that was labeled "progress" or "development" has had as a significant product: impoverishment of land and water, of human beings' ability to sustain self and habitat, and the diminution of Creation as teacher.

We might be quick to point at the enterprise of others. But each of us engages in or plans enterprise at some scale. As I look at my own enterprise, I find myself becoming defensive. "It simply is not *realistic* to place integrity of Creation first," I might reply. "Get real!" I say. But, by this I imply that ecosystems—the support base for all enterprise—are less real than the enterprise; clearly such response is mistaken, lacks discernment. "That would slow me up," I might reply. But I know I will be slowed only if I do not know where I am going; to be guided by a map and destination is not inimical to progress, nor even to speed or efficiency. "But what if I have no goal, except to keep going, and go as fast as I can?" I reply. I find myself caught in a net of my own making. And thus we come to "enterprise."

The Meaning of Enterprise. The dictionary defines enterprise as "a systematic purposeful activity...an undertaking that is difficult, complicated, or risky."[22] In the words of the Oxford English Dictionary, it is a "bold, arduous, or momentous undertaking."[23] Enterprise is purposeful, is directed toward a given end; it is substantial, difficult, and complicated organized activity.

The Goal of Enterprise. If we accept this definition, we ask, "What then is the goal of those enterprises whose operation degrades Creation?" The answer most often is obvious (and is left to the reader). Evaluation will usually find the Precedence Principle violated: wholeness and integrity of Creation is not sought first, but something else. In fairness, we often may correctly say that structures within which it operates leaves it with no other recourse but to degrade Creation—be it church, government, business, or university. But no doubt we also find insufficient effort to reform or replace these structures. Somehow, the integrity of Creation—in its human and creaturely fullness—has not been our goal. Application of the Precedence Principle would find enterprise—economic, governmental, juridical, charitable, ecclesiastical, educational—putting pursuit of wholeness and integrity of Creation first. Its success would be measured by the degree to which it met *this* goal. Such enterprise would be real, earnest, and life would be its goal.[24]

Challenge and Difficulty of Enterprise. Besides being goal-directed, enterprise usually is difficult, complicated, momentous, even risky. It does not simply yield ready-to-use goods in reflex to monetary inputs; it is not a vending machine. Not only has it a goal, but a blueprint for achieving it, a structure that puts the right materials, energy, workers and managers with the right relationships in the right places at the right times doing the right things in the right amounts. If coordination is not sustained, the enterprise may fail. If a component pursues its own ends, and if not discerned and corrected, it may miscarry. Its success is measured by the degree to which it achieves its goal.[25]

Redemptive Enterprise. But in our times, not only must enterprises sustain Creation's integrity, it must win back what was lost, *restore* integrity where degraded, allow Creation to reclaim its self-control and reestablish Creation as teacher. The alternative would be to assume the overwhelming task of Earth management and education—of which we are incapable. The prevalence of impoverishment (embedded in the very fabric of "development" and "progress") means that any enterprise now envisioned must be redemptive. It must undo impoverishment produced and allowed by current enterprise, relieve the biosphere of the relentlessness of exploitation, and allow intrinsic recovery systems to operate. It must be sustained and be sustainable. It must humbly give back to Creation the opportunity and rest necessary to restore, employ, and sustain its intrinsic ability to heal. Redemptive enterprise must in some sense do as a doctor does for a great teacher brought down in battle: establish and maintain the conditions for self-healing so that the patient can be restored to life as a supportive benefactor of life and community.

Enterprise Achieving Reversal of Impoverishment. Enterprise thus must achieve a full reversal of impoverishment. It must give people significant control over life and environment. It must respect and save the means for sustainable households, including, for example, transfer of oral tradition, and maintaining and reestablishing seed and roots of locally adapted stocks. It must protect and provide inheritors with the means to continue as long-standing transmitters of knowledge on sustainable living within particular habitats and ecosystems. It must restore dignity and respect to people sustaining themselves within long-standing cultures; it must protect their lands and habitats for their use and our education.

Risky Enterprise. Undoing impoverishment by restoring and sustaining the integrity of Creation—of people, land, and creatures—is also risky. If enterprise is not truly redemptive, then Creation may be worse off; we may reap the whole world, but lose the integrity of Creation. If we fail to establish a goal with integrity of Creation at its core or fail at putting it into practice, Creation will be less and less effective as a teacher, people will become poorer stewards of family, community, land, and creatures, and we will have fewer means for living rightly on Earth.

The future challenge is enterprise in the fullest sense of its meaning. Not only does it need a definitive and unclouded goal, but it must be a bold, arduous, and momentous undertaking.

From Enterprise to the Meaning of Development. We have prepared the ground and put the seeds of ethics, ecosystems, and enterprise in place. We have found the legal and technical approaches for addressing degradation insufficient and have come to consider an ethics consistent with and supportive of ecosystem principles. We next identified degradations of Creation as impoverishment. We found enterprise to be based necessarily upon these ethics and knowledge of ecosystems. Now it is necessary to discover the meaning of development.

Discovering the Meaning of Development

Development is getting the right things in the right amounts in the right places at the right times with the right relationships. This is its meaning in developmental biology. In organismic development there is no advantage for the brain to grow out of proportion with the kidney. Organs reciprocally serve each other and are scaled accordingly. Thus, proportioned growth and balance is the rule. Furthermore, all components are produced in proper proximity to allow relationships that sustain integrity. Organismic development is also a process of proper timing: some components must be in the context of others at precisely the right times, otherwise development rarely will proceed to maturity. While some components are in place throughout development, others are present only temporarily before they are recycled into raw materials to be used again.

Components also are increased or decreased in size so that one does not overwhelm the other. Growth—positive and negative—is controlled on behalf of the organism. In development of the skeletal system, for example, bone is added by osteoblasts and removed by osteoclasts—specialized cells that redistribute structural strength in response to changing stresses and needs. Sometimes development involves no growth, as in the case of fruit fly embryos which in their early stages increase in quality but not quantity. In biological systems growth subserves development. Failure to do so results from a disorder in which components escape from controls on proportioned growth, allowing them to overtake other components and bring down the whole organism. Such uncontrolled components and their growth are collectively called "cancer."

These descriptions of biological development can be helpful in informing us on human societal development. We will begin by evaluating the difference between development and growth.

The Widespread Confusion of Growth with Development

While people clearly distinguish between growth and development in the human body, they often fail to do so in society. We often hear growth being strongly promoted as though it means development. And those who question urban growth might quickly be labelled "antigrowth"—a pejorative term in society but not in oncology. What we should discern is that it is not possible to be *merely* "progrowth" or "antigrowth." Growth is not something unto itself. In some contexts it is vital, in others, lethal. Thus while we might compliment a child on how much he has physically grown, we would not do the same for a mature adult! We recognize here that development means achieving a kind of balance in which things are rightly proportioned and interconnected—physically, mentally and socially. For children and adults, growth is put into development perspective. But in society we often speak of growth and development as though they mean the same thing—fusing them into a single concept. We even find promotion of this confusion. Ask the question "Who benefits from this confusion?"

What Then Is Development?

The Goal of Development. Development is enterprise, and enterprise always is goal-directed. The critical question for development is "What is its goal? What is its purpose?" Can we know this by observing its outcome, as we might do for an organism or ecosystem? In part the answer is yes, since we can find those examples that satisfy us. But what of urban development, as it is expressed in some of our largest cities? Among its products are increased crime, higher prices, elevated taxes, greater congestion and elevated air pollution. Clearly these were not its stated goals, but they have been achieved nevertheless, even obscuring what may have been intended goals. Often the goal we find was undefined "development" or "growth."

Can our answer be found in the relationship between ethics, ecosystems, and enterprise? Development for its own sake is not development since it has no end in view. Neither is development that results in its own collapse, or destroys its ecosystem support base. Development must be enterprise, and enterprise, as we have seen, must be based upon a goal—a blueprint of what ought to be. It must be based upon an ethic that accords with how the ecosystem of which it is part is sustained and maintains integrity. Sustainable development is enterprise in support of, and supported by, intact, integral, and self-sustaining ecosystems with which it is integrated.

Thus arises our present dilemma. Our ethics are not derived from attempts to assure integrity and sustainability of the ecosystems supporting us. Instead, an enterprise with a different goal dictates our ethics. Rather than ethics guiding enterprise, this enterprise dictates ethics. Our dictum appears to be "what is good for the enterprise is good for Creation." But this is backwards thinking that allows, for example, the market to dictate the meaning of "good"—be that "good" business, "good" investments, or "good" money. Enterprise, unbounded by constraints of stewardship and love of neighbor, society, and ecosystem, can and will bring Creation low. Enterprise without integrity of Creation as its goal will degrade Creation. And so it has: human devastation of Creation has never been greater.

Integrity of Creation as the Goal of Enterprise. In terms of the Precedence Principle, we must first seek wholeness and integrity of Creation, not self-interest. Maximizing conversion of Creation should not be the goal of enterprise. Whatever wealth is gained from Creation should come as a consequence of our care and keeping of it—of diligent work to preserve and restore its integrity. Pursuit and accumulation of wealth as our highest priority will degrade Creation and Creation's wealth and we will all become poorer. But pursuit of Creation's integrity as our first priority will lead to continuing, sustainable, durable wealth measured not only by accumulated goods but by the goodness and integrity of the ecosystems of which we are part.

Development Enterprise: Goal Components. Working from the ethical principles developed earlier, we can derive the content of development's goal. This content can be expressed in parallel with the ethical principles stated earlier, as follows. The goal of development enterprise (integrity of Creation), incorporates:

1. *Reflection*—keeping the Earth, applying nurture and care to the creatures and ecosystems affected by our activities, and holding everything in trust as responsible trustees.
2. *Leadership*—developing and sustaining leadership that works to undo the work of the destroyers of Creation, and does the work of preserving, restoring and nurturing the ecosystems we affect and of which we are part.
3. *Restoration*—providing for rejuvenation, regeneration, and restoration for all components of the ecosystems of which we are a part (both human, and nonhuman) including provision of the necessary time and rest to use its own restorative capacities to refresh, renew, and recreate itself.
4. *Fruitfulness*—incorporating our enjoyment of the fruits of Creation—derived both from people and from nature—without de- grading the fruitfulness and self-sustaining processes of people and nature;

5. *Precedence*—seeking wholeness and integrity of Creation first of all rather than self-interest.

6. *Contentment*—maximizing contentment in a society that clearly discerns contentment from material accumulation.

7. *Action*—enabling people to gain knowledge of how ecosystems work, to gain knowledge of the right, and to act upon this knowledge with openness. This includes opportunity for stewardship over some part of the whole and opportunity for effective, responsible, and substantial participation in democratic processes directed at the integrity of Creation.

Discovering the Meaning of Food Security

Security is the state of being so situated that one is relieved from exposure to danger and placed beyond all hazard of losing.[26] We have noted in the "Degradations of Creation" section at the start of this paper that the capacity of the land to produce food—its fruitfulness—is being degraded. While reasons for such degradation are many and complex, they largely originate in the desire and drive to meet immediate societal needs and wants as a higher priority than ecosystem integrity. In the ethical terms we used earlier this can be described as going beyond enjoyment and use of the fruits of Creation to degrade and destroy its fruitfulness and self-sustaining processes. The ethical principle of fruitfulness is being violated; so are the ecosystem principles upon which this is based. Also being violated is the ethical principle of precedence: we must first seek the wholeness and integrity of Creation, not self-interest; seeking Creation's integrity first brings sustainable wealth.

In a case study in this volume entitled "Missionary Earthkeeping," a number of cases are presented of indigenous people whose cultures are geared to long-term food security rather than maximization of immediate return. These are respectful of the ecosystem and ethical principles we have presented above. Ecosystem-based ethics (Principles 1–7) are basic for general security. Until these principles are applied, as they apparently have been for centuries by many cultures, human society will be at risk; it will experience continued and growing food insecurity.

We have distinguished growth from development, and in the matter of food security we must be careful to do the same. What is needed is not simply more food or more calories. Instead, we need to get the right foods in the right amounts in the right places with the right relationships—in short, we need food security development. We have defined development as enterprise, pointing toward integrity of Creation as its goal. Integrity of Creation is the necessary pre–requisite for achieving food security; without this, food insecurity will be chronic.

Catalysts for Further Thinking

Before coming to a resolution of what has been presented, I offer the following "seeds for thought," which I hope will be helpful in continuing our thinking beyond the content of this paper.

Societal Problems as Reflections of Ourselves. "...nearly all of our societal problems are reflections of ourselves—of what we are in our lifestyles, our culture, our outlook, our vision of life...References to fate, to an inescapable destiny of western civilization, are avenues of escaping our responsibility in history."[27]

Requisites for an Ethical Education. These can be given in three categories, each depending upon the previous one, and each with its important components: (l) awareness (seeing, naming, identifying, locating), (2) appreciation (tolerating, respecting, valuing, esteeming, cherishing), and (3) stewardship (using, restoring, serving, keeping, entrusting).

Development of Human Fulfillment. Our interconnections with oxygen, carbon dioxide, water, foods, wastes, soil, and other creatures must ever be part of our consciousness. If not, we will find that we destroy the very things that give satisfaction, fulfillment, inspiration, spiritual enrichment, life support, and contentment. A community that provides for creatures as well as itself is enriched with life and healthful diversity. Riches and value are not to be found only in banks and possessions.

Sustained Economic Growth. Is sustained economic growth possible within a finite ecosystem? Developmental and ecosystem principles show that growth in quantity is not sustainable; but that the development and growth of quality probably is. The opportunity to raise quality is vast, and already is being realized in reduction of massive library materials to electronic data, with improved reliability and accessibility. By seizing such opportunities our future economies will flourish.

Scientific and Research Institutions. Do our research institutions and researchers work to understand better how the world works in order to keep and restore Creation's integrity? What ethics guide them and to whom do they give service? Should they be constrained from fully serving the goals of justice, peace, and integrity of Creation? Are human scientific resources wasted?

Glasnost, Openness and Disclosure. During a public meeting in Russia in August 1991, the director of the chemical laboratory at Chernobyl Power Station lectured on nuclear power. Wearing a shirt with a nuclear warning, he spoke strongly against nuclear power. Does such "glasnost" or "openness" exist elsewhere in industry even in "democratic" countries?

Word Security. Once we agree on what must be done, and have it in writing, we find among ourselves those who selfishly benefit from turning the meaning of words to their antithesis. Consider: sustainable growth, business community, the global village, the human family, intelligence, security.

Notes

1. "Creation" is the term I use throughout this paper for the system of interacting human cultures and environment and the components of this system. I do this quite deliberately since we currently have no other comprehensive term that embraces both human beings and nature. The words "environment" and "nature," while widely used, are not acceptable alternatives since they lead one to think of human beings as separate entities. Later in the paper I use the words "biosphere" and "ecosystem," both of which I take as components of Creation.

2. The following are some key references for each of the seven degradations given here:
   a. Alteration of planetary energy exchange: J. Anderson, D. Toohey, and W. Brune, "Free Radicals Within the Antarctic Vortex: The Role of CFCs in Antarctic Ozone Loss," *Science* 251 (1991): 39. B. Bolin et al., eds., *The Greenhouse Effect, Climatic Change and Ecosystems* (New York: John Wiley, 1986).
   b. Land degradation: S. Anderson et al., "Estimating Soil Erosion After 100 Years of Cropping on Sanborn Field," *Journal of Soil and Water Conservation* 45 no. 6 (1990): 641. T. Plaut, "Urban Expansion and the Loss of Farmland in the U.S.: Implications for the Future," *American Journal of Agricultural Economics* (Aug 1980): 537.
   c. Deforestation and habitat destruction: D. Given, "Conserving Botanical Diversity on a Global Scale," *Ann. Missouri Botanical Gardens* 77 (1990): 48. R. Houghton, "The Global Effects of Tropical Deforestation," *Environmental Science Technology* 24 (1990): 414.
   d. Species extinction: S. Geer, "One-Fourth of the World's Plant and Animal Species May Face Extinction," *Environmental Conservation* 16 (1989): 372.

e. Water degradation: M. Leistra and J. Boesten, "Pesticide Contamination of Groundwater in Western Europe, Agriculture," *Ecosystems and Environment* 26 (1989): 369. J. Maurits la Riviere, "Threats to the World's Water," *Scientific American* (Sept 1989): 80. D. Moody, "Groundwater Contamination in the U.S.," *Journal of Soil and Water Conservation* 45 no. 2 (1990): 170.

f. Global toxification: E. Atlas and C. Giam, "Global Transport of Organic Pollutants: Ambient Concentrations in the Remote Marine Atmosphere," *Science* 211 (1980): 163. P. Larsson et al., "Atmospheric Transport of Persistent Pollutants Governs Uptake by Holarctic Terrestrial Biota," *Environmental Science Technology* 24 (1990): 1599. K. Reinhardt and D. Wodarg, "Transport of Selected Organochlorine Compounds Over the Sea," *Journal of Aerosol Science* 19 (1988): 1251.

g. Human and cultural degradation: N. Awa, "Participation and Indigenous Knowledge in Rural Development," *Knowledge* 10 (1989): 304. Julie S. Denslow and Christine Padoch, *People of the Tropical Rain Forest* (Berkeley: University of California Press, 1988). S. Gliessman, E. Garcia, and A. Amador, "The Ecological Basis for the Application of Traditional Agricultural Technology in the Management of Tropical Agro-Ecosystems," *Agro-Ecosystems* 7 (1981): 173. M. Oldfield and J. Alcorn, "Conservation of Traditional Agro-Ecosystems," *BioScience* 37 (Mar 1987): 199.

3. An example of a textbook developed for this purpose is the one by Mike W. Martin and Roland Schinzinger, *Ethics in Engineering* (New York: McGraw-Hill, 1989).

4. Quotations from *The Asissi Declarations: Messages on Man & Nature from Buddhism, Christianity, Hinduism, Islam & Judaism* (World Wildlife Fund, 1986). Authors are the Venerable Lungrig Namgyal Rinpoche, Abbot of Gyuto Tantric University (Buddhism), Father Lanfranco Serrini, Minister General of the Franciscan Order (Christian), His Excellency Dr. Karan Singh, President, Hindu Virat Samaj (Hindu), His Excellency Dr. Abdullah Omar Nasseef, Secretary General of the Muslim World League (Muslim), and Rabbi Arthur Hertzberg, Vice-President of the World Jewish Congress (Jewish). For additional similar material, see Calvin B. DeWitt, "The Religious Foundations of Ecology," in *The Mother Earth Handbook*, ed. Judith Scherff (New York: Continuum Publishing Co., 1991), 248.

5. To the extent that the principles presented in this paper help readers understand this basic scientific knowledge, it is for the good. But the principles should not be used as a substitute for gaining further information. Neither should their inadequacy be used to build a caricature of science that makes it less substantial than it is in fact.

6. This definition is quoted directly from, and the definition of the first principle is based upon, W. C. Allee et al., *Principles of Animal Ecology* (Philadelphia: W. B. Saunders Co., 1949), 728.

7. For a good introduction to ecosystems and their functions see G. Tyler Miller, *Living in the Environment: An Introduction to Environmental Science*, 6th ed. (Belmont, CA: Wadsworth, 1990).

8. While basing these principles upon an understanding of ecosystems, I exercised control over their content and selection by whether they were in some sense supportable by a long-standing system of ethics. The system I selected is one that has a more than three thousand-year history, and has a well-preserved written record. It is the ethical system of the ancient Hebrew people whose record spans the period from some three thousand to two thousand years ago, and the derivative Christian ethical system whose record comes from the first century A.D. Specific references to textual materials are given in the notes. The hypothesis that I employed in this work was that an ancient tradition with an ethical system persisting into modern times may have ecological principles that have helped sustain it, and thus might be broadly useful in modern society.

9. This Reflection Principle (or Keeping Principle) is a long-standing one. In the Torah, the Aaronic blessing, "The Lord bless you and keep you..." (Num. 6:24–26) uses the same word for "keep" (shamar) as is used in God's stated purpose for human beings, to keep and take care of (shamar) the Garden (Gen. 2:15). Reinforcing this is use of the Hebrew word "abad" in Gen. 2:15 (to serve, for example, to till), translated as "to work" in the New International Version Bible. In the Geneva Bible (1560) Gen. 2:15 is given, "Then the Lord God toke the man, and put him into the garden of Eden, that he might dresse it and kepe it." The "dominion passage" (Gen. 1:26–28) can be seen as supporting this principle, by observing that dominion ceases if that which is ruled is destroyed; furthermore this passage describes people as imaging God, who is the one who "makes springs pour water into the ravines...They give water to all the beasts of the field... The birds of the air nest by the waters; they sing among its branches...the earth is satisfied by the fruit of his work" (Ps. 104:10–13). Thus, we can conclude, the Earth should also be satisfied by the fruit of human work. The concept of dominion as service ("abad" in Gen. 2:15) is reinforced in the Christian tradition (Phil. 2:5–8).

10. The Leadership Principle in the Christian tradition can be stated as, "We must be disciples of the Last Adam, not of the First Adam." This comes from the teaching that people are part of a lineage that has fallen short of the glory of God (Rom. 3:23). "But," affirms this scripture, "Christ has indeed been raised from the dead...as in Adam all die, so in Christ all will be made alive" (1 Cor. 15:20–22). The importance of this comes clear in that it is through Him that all things are reconciled (Col. 1:19–20). As disciples of the One, "by whom all things were made, and through whom all things hold together," (John 1:3; Col. 1:16–17) people participate in undoing the work of the first Adam, bringing restoration and reconciliation to *all things,* doing the tasks the First Adam failed to accomplish (compare John 1 & Col. 1; 1 Corinthians 15 & Rom. 5; Isa. 43:18–21, Isa. 65 & Col. 1:19–20; 5:17–21).

11. The Fruitfulness Principle: The book of Genesis relates how the abundant gifts and fruitfulness of God's Creation did not satisfy; in their pressing Creation, its fruitfulness may be degraded or destroyed. Ezekiel warns, "Is it not enough for you to feed on the good pasture?

Must you also trample the rest of your pasture with your feet? Is it not enough for you to drink clear water? Must you also muddy the rest with your feet?" (Ezek. 34:18; see also Deut. 20:19; 22:6–7). As people are expected to be fruitful, so is the rest of Creation: "Let the water teem with living creatures, and let birds fly above the earth and across the expanse of the sky...Be fruitful and increase in number and fill the water in the seas, and let the birds increase on the earth" (Gen. 1:20–21). With these words, the Creator lavishes blessing upon the creatures, calling forth their fruitfulness, providing blessed impetus to their biological and ecological development, and divinely empowering them to bring fulfilling completeness to the Earth. And thus Isaiah warns: "Woe to you who add house to house and join field to field till no space is left and you live alone in the land" (Isa. 5:8). Expansion of human developments may not be at the expense of fruitfulness of the rest of Creation. Moreover, people are expected to prevent extinction of the creatures, both economic and uneconomic, even at tremendous cost, as in the case of Noah (Gen. 6:9–9:17).

12. The Restoration Principle for those traditions that respect the Torah (Judaism, Islam, and Christianity), can be stated: "We must not press Creation relentlessly, but must provide for its Sabbath rests." The Torah teaches that, as human beings and animals are to be given their sabbaths, so also must the land be given its sabbath rests (Exod. 23:10–12). People, land, and creatures must not be relentlessly pressured. "If you follow My decrees...I will send you rain in its season, and the ground will yield its crops and the trees of the field their fruit" (Lev. 26:3). Otherwise, the land will be laid waste, only then to "have the rest it did not have during the sabbaths you lived in it" (Lev. 26:34–35)!

13. The *Report of the Pre-Assembly Consultation on Subtheme I,* "Giver of Life—Sustain Your Creation!" held in Malaysia, May 12–20 (Geneva, Switzerland: World Council of Churches, 1990) makes an important contribution to this principle: "At Kuala Lumpur, we discovered that our theological work gives rise to a new vision—yet one with ancient roots imbedded in the biblical tradition—concerning the pathways to a hopeful and sustainable future for the world...Out of the rich variety of biblical material, beginning with Genesis and ending with Revelation, that could guide our vision we would like to draw special attention to the concept of Shabbat (the Sabbath), Sabbatical and Jubilee Year...On Shabbat, all divisions, separations and hierarchies among human beings are relinquished and an integral community of resting, adoring, and worshipping is established which also comprises non-human life...Shabbat reminds us that time, the realm of being, is not just a commodity, but has a quality of holiness, which resists our impulse to control, command, and oppress. In Genesis 2, God's creation does not culminate in the creation of human beings but in the rest of Shabbat and in contemplation and appreciation of all. This close unity of social and ecological reconciliation, restoration, and renewal becomes even more clear in the concepts of Sabbatical and Jubilee Year. In the seventh year, even the earth can rest, poor and wild beasts can eat from it, whereas slaves are freed. In the 50th

year, however, this vision of an overall eco-social restoration is extended to the land: a redistribution of land property and an overall liberation is meant to recreate a just and equitable society (Exod. 23; Lev. 25). Thus, the biblical concept of Shabbat joins social justice to environmental stewardship, and law to mercy, to create a model of harmony for all spheres of life."

14. The Precedence Principle (or Priority Principle) is expressed in the Christian tradition in its most widely used prayer: "This, then is how you should pray: 'Our Father in heaven, hallowed be Your name, Your kingdom come, Your will be done on earth...'" (Matt. 6:9–10). The Scriptures show how tempting it is to follow the example of those who accumulate great gain to Creation's detriment. But they also assure people: "Trust in the Lord and do good; dwell in the land and enjoy safe pasture... Those who hope in the Lord will inherit the land" (Ps. 37; Matt. 5:5). Obtaining food, water and clothing—fulfillment of human needs—is a *consequence*, not of seeking these things directly, but of seeking God's kingdom (Matt. 6:33).

15. The Contentment Principle is supported by the prayer "Turn my heart to Your statutes and not toward selfish gain" (Ps. 119:36) and by description of what constitutes true human gain: "...godliness with contentment" (1 Tim. 6:6–21; Heb. 13:5). This is set against the biblical observation that the fruitfulness, grace, and gifts of Creation did not satisfy (Gen. 3–11), resulting in disobedience to the law, doing Creation "one better," making things "bigger than life."

16. The *Report of the Pre-Assembly Consultation on Subtheme I*, "Giver of Life—Sustain Your Creation!" held in Kuala Lumpur, Malaysia, May 12–20 (Geneva, Switzerland: World Council of Churches, 1990) puts it this way: "This includes a new vision of community and sharing. Stories like those of the *manna* in the desert (Exod. 16) tell us that the bread distributed for need and not by greed is the only bread that can sustain life. We sincerely believe that the food we eat while our neighbor is hungry, and the wealth we consume at the expense of others, separate us from the realm of life and have self-destroying effects. Our vision is that those with enough material goods start to look for fulfillment in spiritual life, and that those having economic and political power make decisions based on the needs of all of creation, leading to a fuller life for all."

17. The Action Principle is supported by scriptural teachings that knowing God's requirements for stewardship is not enough; hearing, discussing, singing, and contemplating the Scriptures is insufficient. They must be practiced, or they do absolutely no good. The hard saying of Scripture is this: We hear from our neighbors, "Come and hear the message that has come from the Lord." And they come, "but they do not put them into practice. With their mouths they express devotion, but their hearts are greedy for unjust gain. Indeed, to them you are nothing more than one who sings love songs with a beautiful voice and plays an instrument well, for they hear your words but do not put them into practice" (Ezek. 33:30–32; Luke 6:46–49).

18. Aldo Leopold, "A Land Ethic,"in *A Sand County Almanac*, (New York:

Oxford University Press, 1949), 224.

19. From the *Report of the Pre-Assembly Consultation on Subtheme I,* "Giver of Life—Sustain Your Creation!" held in Kuala Lumpur, Malaysia, May 12–20 (Geneva, Switzerland: World Council of Churches, 1990), 10.

20. World Council of Churches "Giver of Life," *Report.*

21. From hand-written notes recorded by the author from the oral presentation on the Natural History of the Volga River by Russian physicist, Irene Erevula. This presentation was given at the conference on "Christianity and Ecology in Russia" conducted on the cruise ship, Fyodor Dostoevsky, a conference sponsored by the Soviet "Save Peace and Nature Association" and the North Amerian Conference on Christianity and Ecology. Volga River, Russia, August 25, 1991.

22. *Webster's Seventh New Collegiate Dictionary,* s. v. "enterprise."

23. *The Compact Edition of the Oxford English Dictionary,* s. v. "enterprise."

24. It may not be clear to some that the integrity of Creation is a worthy goal, due to confusion of our ideas and models of reality. It is common in recent times to view nature as something to be transformed to match our own model or idea—something we have to a large extent been able to do. But we are making two very significant discoveries: (1) that it is beyond our capability to do so in many areas—for example, comprehensive management of global circulations and world weather patterns; and (2) that, more importantly, it is beyond desirability—many things in this world are better left to their own management systems so people are free to do other things. Thus increasingly we transform our ideas in accord with the principles upon which ecosystems are based and upon related ethical principles.

25. The complexity and challenge of the enterprise needed to achieve integrity of Creation is not as impossible as it first seems. While remaining challenging and complex, our enterprise is made possible by the rejuvenating and self-regulating quality of ecosystems themselves. Our enterprise thus will include responding as a military doctor does to the wounded, by (1) removing the patient from battle to eliminate the human produced conditions that continue the process of degradation, and then (2) providing for the conditions in which self-healing and self-controlling processes can operate fully to bring self-restoration. This of course makes our enterprise no less important; it makes it urgent, but brings focus on conditions that bring degradation, and conditions required for self-restoration. For an introduction to this, see DeWitt, C. B. "Let it Be: A Wetland Scientist and Restorationist Reflects on the Value of Waiting." *Restoration and Management Notes* 7 no. 2 (1989): 80.

26. See definition of "secure," *Webster's Seventh New Collegiate Dictionary.*

27. Bob Goudzwaard, *Capitalism and Progress: A Diagnosis of Western Society,* trans Josina Van Nuys Zylstra. (Grand Rapids: Eerdmans, 1979) 247. Originally published as *Kapitalisme en Vooruitgang* (Assen, Netherlands: Gorcum, 1978).

CHAPTER TWO

PEOPLE-CENTERED DEVELOPMENT, DEMOCRACY AND THE ENVIRONMENT
Towards a Sustainable Development Alternative
Through the Transformation of Agriculture

Atherton E. Martin

*Atherton E. Martin, former Minister of Agriculture of the Caribbean
nation of Dominica and former general secretary of the 2,500 strong
Dominican Farmers Union, introduces us to an alternative development model that puts the poor people who produce food, particularly
women, indigenous folk and the landless, at the center of policy efforts to promote food security and land conservation. Martin speaks
from the heart and from seven years of experience working with small
farmers on his island to establish production cooperatives and develop
new food crops and marketing systems. He paints a convincing
picture in which change trickles up, and magic lies in local efforts of
committed individuals, not in international financial and commodities markets.*

THE PHYSICAL BASIS FOR SURVIVAL, development and human life itself is
found in the natural and social systems that allow the original products of nature to be converted into the goods and services essential to
life. The process and progress of human culture is both a result and a
determining factor in the exercise of the power to make that life-
supporting conversion.[1]

Where the exercise of that power is driven by the need to accumulate material wealth, any activity, use of time, or energy flow that does
not result in the creation of more material wealth or cannot be measured in terms of money is considered useless and expendable. By the
same token, any activity that results in the generation of wealth is
considered acceptable, regardless of the impact on humans or the
environment.

By the year 2000, if present trends continue, one-third of the world's productive land will have turned to dust, one million species will be extinct, and the world's climate will be irreparably changed.[2]

The continuing deterioration of global ecosystems reflects the tendency of current development approaches to erode vital natural resources to the point where it is no longer possible to sustain the most rudimentary levels of subsistence living.[3] Over the past four decades, these approaches have been vigorously pursued in the newly independent states of Africa, the Caribbean, Asia and parts of Latin America where loans from the World Bank, the International Monetary Fund and other major donors have fueled this destructive path to economic growth.[4]

The full impact of the policies and programs implemented during this period is directly felt by the poor in a variety of ways: loss of access to land and other productive resources; falling employment and declining wages; and the collapse of essential services in the areas of health, housing and education. Resources are diverted to repaying foreign debts and buying imported luxury goods. In the critical area of food, policies and programs to support food production for domestic consumption are by-passed in favor of expanding investment in production for export. Formerly food self-sufficient communities are now dependent upon imports and foreign aid. Persistent hunger and malnutrition have increased dramatically, with the greatest burden falling on women and young children.

In the 1980s, one of the countries which was held up as a model of the success of privatization and export led growth was Jamaica. In order to appreciate the significance of this claim in the context of women, it is useful to recall that during this period of "recovery," 35 percent of the households in Jamaica were headed by women who parented children, cared for the elderly, managed households, and participated in community affairs, in addition to contributing as producers and wage earners.

Throughout the decade, in spite of vigorous adherence to the dictates of structural adjustment, unemployment among women in Jamaica ranged between 60 and 70 percent. As cutbacks in expenditures on health services resulted in sharp increases in the incidence of gastroenteritis and malnutrition among children, women were forced to devote more time to home care, even while holding on to low-paying jobs in one of the two growth points of the economy, export processing zones.

The paradox of such a situation is that although it is the labor of women that is clearly essential to the production of low-cost goods for export, and hence, to the success of this export led approach, it is the productivity of women that is most severely undermined by this growth-driven strategy. In Jamaica, as in many other countries, this paradox is conceived when a strong export thrust is combined with cutbacks in health, transportation, and education services, low wages, unsafe conditions at the workplace, and the failure to value the reproductive labor of women in their homes and communities as an ongoing contribution to growth and economic recovery.

In spite of compelling evidence of the negative impact of this development approach on the economy, the environment, and the people of the South, many bilateral and multilateral aid agencies continue to advocate and finance these same policies and programs that virtually act as midwife to the human misery that abounds in many of these countries.

Recent events in eastern Europe and the Soviet Union seem to suggest that the centrally planned approach to economics has failed to deliver the goods and services essential to the well-being of the people. The dramatic events there certainly reveal the widespread dissatisfaction of the population with the performance of those economies.

These same events, however, seem to have clouded the fact that for decades (not months or years), the people in most countries of the Third World have expressed vigorous dissatisfaction with the failure of the capital, free-market approach to producing goods and services accessible to the population. However, the claims of 'success' for this approach persist despite the growing poverty, hunger, famine, war, and environmental destruction that characterize the numerous countries pursuing this model.

This model is the one now advocated as holding the answer to the crisis ridden countries of Eastern Europe and the Soviet Union. It seems that the disasters of underdevelopment in the South are about to be replicated in the North. It seems that the voices of the poor in the South still have not been heard. It seems that the disasters wrought by capital driven growth, foreign aid, green revolution agriculture, trade liberalization, privatization and structural adjustment are still being ignored.

Those who seek answers to the misery of persistent poverty wherever it occurs are now challenged to look beyond the drama of falling walls, falling bombs, falling governments and falling leaders. We are challenged to get to the roots of the deep-seated conceptual and structural constraints which still lie in the path of equitable and sustainable development.

The purpose of this paper is to consider how people can transform

dependent agricultural economies into more self-reliant and self-sufficient systems while at the same time halting environmental degradation and promoting broad-based, equitable growth. The paper
examines ways of achieving this transformation through a process
that is characterized by the increased involvement of local people in
making that transition. The paper begins with a brief description of the
impact of current policies on agriculture in the South; makes a case for
a different approach to the development of agriculture; presents a
conceptual framework for that approach; describes what an alternative agriculture might look like; identifies several critical factors to be
considered in making the transition to that alternative; and proposes a
series of next steps to be taken at the local, national, and international
levels in the process of shaping a sustainable development alternative.

Impact on Agriculture

Dominated by the economies and policies of the North, many
formerly self-sufficient regions of the South have become dependent
upon outside resources. A major feature of these dependent agricultural systems is the production of export (cash) crops rather than food
crops for domestic consumption.

The transition from self-sufficiency to dependency is related to
several critical factors that must be addressed in the creation of any
alternative approach. These include:

- the well financed and aggressive thrust of research institutions in promoting Green Revolution techniques, which are
  expensive and often inappropriate for conditions under
  which most small, poor farmers operate;[5]
- global commercial policies that use pricing, customs,
  phytosanitary and other regulations to discriminate against
  traditional crops in favor of hybrid cash crops in international trade;[6]
- the pressures from international lending agencies to collect
  hard currency payments on debt;[7] and
- the failure of local governments to involve farmers in plans
  for improving agriculture.[8]

The demand for cash to buy imported industrial and consumer
products and the conversion of lands from food to cash crops, com-
pounded by the need to feed growing populations, has increased
pressure on traditional farming systems and forced marginal lands

into production as farmers try to produce enough to eat and to sell. Fallow periods, multiple cropping, and planting and maintaining trees to protect against soil erosion have been progressively abandoned and replaced by the increased use of hybrid seed, chemical fertilizer, pure stand cropping, annual replanting, deep tilling and other Green Revolution modes of agriculture.

The very technologies and systems of modern agriculture, which were heralded as the means for resolving the problems of hunger and satisfying the demands of international trade, have contributed to the degradation of soils and pollution of the water systems so essential to sustain agricultural production. In the final analysis, this high-tech approach to agriculture, that was demanded by the promoters and financiers of export led growth, has led to sharp declines in the availability of food for local consumption, increased malnutrition among children, and the steady displacement of systems of traditional farming and the farmers who had knowledge of those systems.[9]

In macro economic terms, this high-input system of production for export has attacked the very roots of agricultural sustainability by :[10]
- promoting the notion of yield maximization in the short term without regard to soil fertility and other longer-term environmental consequences;
- displacing rural workers with capital intensive husbandry practices, such as the use of herbicides;
- marginalizing women from food production by reducing the amount of land left for growing vegetables and raising animals for home use after the best lands were used by male farmers to produce cash crops for export;
- abandoning polyculture in favor of monoculture;
- abandoning local varieties of crops in favor of introduced hybrids;
- failing to promote or finance the use of locally produced raw materials in agro-industry and in other sectors like tourism; and
- promoting the international marketplace as the final determinant of efficiency, resource allocation and overall economic priorities.

The response to this crisis has been to administer more of the very same medicine that caused the crisis in the first place.[11] The threat to people and environment has therefore been exacerbated policies that attempt to counter dropping commodity prices by extending the area under cultivation with cash crops. This means the removal of forests, the displacement of forest dwellers, the increased use of toxic chemicals, the loss of biogenetic diversity, the replacement of food crops with cash crops, and the increased dependence of entire economies on fragile markets.

The Search for an Alternative

Current development approaches are rapidly bringing us to the point where the capacity of many regions to grow sufficient food to feed themselves is seriously threatened and may already be at the point where the land's capacity to support life is stretched to the limit.[12] There is no choice but to search for alternatives.

Something is radically wrong with a system when higher crop yields are accompanied by greater hunger and starvation because less food is available for local consumption. Similarly, when an economic strategy is predicated on greater dependence on export markets at the same time that the prices of commodities sold on these markets is in steady decline, resulting in less export earnings from increased production, it can only be concluded that the object is the calcul-ated impoverishment of the countries pursuing that strategy.

The deepening crisis in agriculture and in the global economic and political systems has stimulated renewed thinking and action about alternative development. This search for a different way is driven by a rejection of the prevailing systems of governance which tolerate (if not promote) the deprivation of large numbers of people as a basis for economic growth. This search for a new path is also driven by the growing awareness that current approaches to resource use not only deny people a chance to have a say in their own lives, but in many ways deprive people of their livelihoods by destroying the natural resource base that is essential to life itself. [13]

For millions of poor rural people all over the world, therefore, the search for an alternative is often a search for survival. This search has been going on for decades and involves members of society in seeking a role for themselves in shaping and operating systems of production and governance that respond to their social and economic needs. One of the main lessons to be drawn from this ongoing struggle is that while there are no single or simple approaches to meeting all human needs, strategies that can address those needs will have to be drawn from and respond to the lived experiences of the people.

A Conceptual Framework for the Alternative Economy

Let's agree that the fundamental purpose of human activity is the satisfaction of human life needs and that the natural ecosystem is the primary and most fundamental asset upon which the satisfaction of these needs is premised. Then the goal of sustainable development is to ensure the skillful combination of human resources and natural resources to meet those needs in ways that would not destroy either the humans or the natural resources.

Conversely, if the goal of alternative development is wealth accumulation and profit maximization, the "free market" will discount both the human and natural resources in the economic equation whenever either interferes with these goals. This means, therefore, not only a new mindset that places human and natural resources as top priorities, but new ways of viewing the interaction and interdependence between the two, new ways of blending the two for more sustained output, new ways of distributing use of, and benefit from, the use of resources, and new ways and tools to measure our performance. This new approach must challenge the trickle-down model that uses only monetized benchmarks of performance, and it must challenge the nonconsultative, nondemocratic process by which development policies are formulated.

The path to an alternative economy begins with and emerges from the experiences of the local population. This thesis maintains that these local experiences contain the rudiments of the vision, the values, the guidelines, the expertise, the technology and the systems of popular participation that are pivotal to a sustainable development alternative.[14]

Four basic features of an alternative economy emerge from popular experiences. These can form the basis of a conceptual framework against which policies and programs can be measured. The features are:

1. participation, which refers to enabling people to use their knowledge and expertise to improve their well-being and to shape policies and programs;
2. self-reliance, which includes creating structures with resources that enhance community well-being and decrease dependence on external inputs, technology and markets through using available local expertise and raw materials to meet people's needs;
3. equity, which connotes access to economic resources and services matched by access to legal and constitutional rights and privileges; it is accompanied by accepting the responsibility to

contribute to the economic, social and environmental well-being
of the community; and
4. sustainability, which speaks to the capacity and willingness of
   all sectors to be involved in producing goods and services in
   ways that enhance the natural resource base and leave it in an
   improved condition for use by future generations.

These four features, while distinct, overlap and interact with each
other in the process of shaping an alternative economy.

What an Alternative Economy Might Look Like

The overarching goal of an alternative development model is the
creation of an economy in which the participation of people in the
economic, social and political life of their communities becomes the
most critical factor in the systems and institutions that will address the
needs of those people.

In the case of agriculture, for example, where one of the overriding
aims is food security, the productivity, stability and sustainability of
farm systems should allow for increased production without threatening the environment or the public well-being. These methods should
also promote the economic and social self-reliance of the community.

In the process of assuring food security, other structural problems
of the economy are also addressed. New agro-industries are supplied
with local raw materials, opening up new jobs in the rural and urban
areas. Economic diversification and modernization of production are
increasingly dependent upon local resources, expertise, markets and
support services so that a truly self-reliant economic option begins to
unfold.

As this alternative economy becomes focused on ensuring that the
needs of the local population are safely and sustainably met, the
economy itself becomes increasingly dependent upon the involvement and the expertise of local people. Networks of popular organizations already working at the community level should have an
opportunity to become the vehicles for transferring the experience of
people's participation in the construction of a self-reliant, sustainable
and equitable economy from the local to the national level, and then to
the regional level.

The alternative economy is characterized by the following features:
1. Decision-making institutions involve representatives from a
   broad cross section of organizations, including the public and

private sectors, as well as community-based groups that work with and represent the poor. (The existence of even highly sophisticated systems of parliamentary mechanisms has not necessarily ensured such broad participation, and certainly does not preclude establishing popular mechanisms of dialogue and decision making that include forms drawn from relevant local traditions of consultation.)

2. Choices about goals of the society are based on the supremacy of the people and on meeting their real needs. This means, for example, that in selecting the means for achieving economic growth, the impact on jobs, wages, health and safety, security, productivity, efficiency and equity in sharing benefits and costs are taken into account.

3. In the interest of conserving and enhancing the natural resource base of the economy, and thereby safeguarding the economic future of the society, the emphasis is on sustaining rather than maximizing economic growth.

4. Production is geared to the task of meeting local needs for goods, services and jobs, but certain sectors are also organized to generate trade with neighboring countries.

5. Food security is addressed by making hard choices about land use and land reform that ensure food producers access to adequate resources. Choices are made about the use of technology in food production that enhance the quality of the product, reduce dependence on imported inputs, lower environmental costs and make use of locally generated expertise and raw materials.

6. In the case of agriculture, research, and other services, we have the task of striking a balance between traditional and imported technology, working closely with farmers to ensure relevancy to local needs.

7. The choice between a) consumer-based industrialization and b) agro-based enterprises, using local raw materials, is made, as is the choice between c) urban expansion and d) integrated rural development.

8. The role of the state as a major actor in economic decision making is assessed in the light of its success in developing key institutions that can effect positive change. The relationship between the state and grassroots community organizations reflects the strengths of both sectors as a wide range of perceptions are brought together to focus on issues of common concern.

9. Global issues of trade, aid, debt and structural adjustment are

seen as major constraints to the emergence of this model, and attempts at building an economy that serves people is seen as a repudiation of the model that has failed to deliver the benefits of growth to millions.

The following section describes in greater detail selected efforts of community organizations, women, farmers, youth and others who are applying these elements to their daily battles for survival and, in the process, are contributing to the shaping of an alternative approach to development.

Making the Transition to an Alternative

In setting out a route to local and national food security within the context of alternative development, a beginning is recognizing and accepting that farmers' knowledge, skills and resources can provide a sound and dynamic base for food security. Until recently, the vast knowledge of farmers, fisherpeople, forest dwellers, etc. was discounted or actively discredited by colonial authorities and postcolonial agricultural and development specialists. Over the past decade, people have reclaimed their rights to their own culture and knowledge systems, and outsiders have begun to document the local knowledge around farming systems.[15]

Popular Knowledge

Farmers' knowledge involves a deep understanding of both macro and micro ecosystems. For example, on the macro side, farmers in the Sahel anticipate the onset of the rains (and thus their planting preparation) by observing the changes of the leaves of trees, which are influenced by changes in climatic pressure and humidity. On the micro side, farmers in the mountains of Peru use the different climatic zones over 1,000–1,500 meters vertical elevation to plant various crops.

The cropping technique helps illustrate the value of farmers' knowledge. Intercropping has long been practiced by rural people, although over the past forty years research scientists and extension workers have actively sought to discourage intercropping as unproductive and unsightly. Intercropping offers many advantages in crop production: it reduces risk to insect or weather conditions that may affect one or more crops, but not all; it spreads out the availability of crops over a long growing season as some crops ripen earlier than others; it reduces erosion; it enhances soil quality, composition and sustainability; and it contributes to pest reduction.

Following are additional examples of how participation and using existing knowledge can improve agricultural practices:

Research and Technology Adoption. The key is to use farmers (in conjunction with researchers) in seed trials, pest management, etc. Both individuals and groups of farmers are ready experimenters, capable of pragmatic and precise testing. In western Kenya, households have recently adopted a yam variety from Uganda which requires less land and labor—major considerations for rural people —than sweet potatoes or potatoes. The opportunity to reduce the costs of maintaining research centers and make experiments immediately relevant to local needs is clearly evident by having scientists and extension agents work closely with farmers.[16]

Seed Multiplication. The availability of seed is a constant barrier for farmers who must plant in a timely manner to assure highest yields. Farmers regularly select the best seeds from previous crops for use in subsequent years and are familiar with selection and breeding procedures. Village-based seed production, using local labor, can be done at one-tenth the cost to consumers of hybrid seed sold through commercial channels. The seeds would be improved composite varieties, would be more adapted and responsive to local environments, more readily and reasonably available than hybrids. Local communities would be adding value to their production in the form of seed sales, thereby stimulating their economies. Any potential shortfall in levels of production currently obtained from hybrid seeds would be made up by higher yields from timely planting and seed responsiveness to local conditions.[17]

Farmers—particularly women—regularly bring wild plants into their farms, sometimes for domestication. In many countries, the sale of seeds from wild/domesticated plants was an important household activity which also served to expand both genetic diversity and local incomes.

Pesticide Use. The cost of commercial pesticides can be substantially reduced by promoting intercropping, especially with crops that provide a natural deterrent, and use of pesticides prepared from local plants. In Kerala State, India, *neem* cake offers a natural control against soil-borne pests (it also contains long-valued medicinal qualities). An "informal marketing" of *neem* exists to growers of specialized fruit and vegetable crops. Resource-poor farmers use *neem* leaves to protect grains during storage. In northern Ghana and other Sahel areas, farmers favor growing under or near the Acacia albida tree because striga, a parasitic weed common throughout the region, does not grow near the trees.[18]

Genetic Diversity: Farmers assure food security through maintaining a diversity of crops. Four hundred varieties of potato have been identified in Peru; over twenty varieties of rice are found in Sierra Leone and Thailand. That diversity offers tremendous opportunities for further experimentation, for expanding food security, for adaption for medicinal and other uses. Also, the range of varieties suggests that the high costs of agricultural research stations can be dramatically reduced by looking more closely at adapting existing varieties rather than developing totally new ones.

Self-Reliance

The power of self-reliance is a crucial concept in the democratization of development. The ability of communities to care for their members and to promote open debate and decision making are symbolic models not easily ignored. For example, in Negros, the Philippines, sugar workers who lost their jobs in the mid-1980s have successfully negotiated with landowners for tracts of unused land upon which the workers produce food crops.[19] Kerala is one of the poorest states in India; yet, sustained popular pressure has created programs that use indigenous resources to reduce illiteracy and malnutrition, and to expand land reform.

Communities have a variety of organizational structures that support their vast knowledge around food security. Those structures provide an alternative to the costly and inflexible bureaucratic approach of most state and development agency systems. Local organizations are an essential component in promoting alternatives, as they represent the means by which local people can mobilize themselves for equitable and sustainable development.

Agrarian Reform. Access to adequate land and its productive use for human needs is a key component in many popular struggles. It has become the base for pursuing equity and self-reliance in many societies. Peasants' demands for land have been driving Zimbabwe's land redistribution program. With greater access to land and supportive national policies, Zimbabwe's peasant farmers have laid the basis for food security (including exports) for the country. In Central America, land and food security were at the base of Nicaragua's revolution, and are central to the struggles in El Salvador, Guatemala and Honduras.

There is an extensive history of land reform experiences to draw upon, such as those in Mexico and China earlier this century. Similarly, agrarian reform in Eritrea has involved changes in land tenûre and farmers' organization in order to use land for local self-reliance. Women, in particular, have gained greater access to land by increasing their activism in village assemblies.

Labor Sharing. Most societies have several labor-sharing structures to facilitate work in a timely manner or to increase available household labor resources. Women's work groups exist across Africa, and some have been formalized in recent years with external program support. The Green Movement in Kenya has built upon women's agricultural and environmental knowledge to promote tree planting, income generation and community development.

Labor sharing at a more complex level is seen in cooperatives. One of the major examples is in the Green Zones in Mozambique. Begun by women around Maputo, the capital, as spontaneous suburban vegetable gardens in the years after independence, the gardens grew rapidly as more women joined to more effectively organize their labor. Joint buying of inputs and joint marketing followed. Cooperatives were formed and remain active, managed primarily for and by women. In less than a decade, the Green Zone concept jumped from an informal food production system to a major component of national policy on food security.[20]

Savings and Credit. Popular and informal savings and credit networks exist and function in most societies. Numerous savings and credit networks facilitate marketing relations in West Africa, often involving large amounts of money. The Grameen Bank in Bangladesh has received vast publicity about its small-scale credit program for low-income people, especially women.

NGOs play a significant role in credit provision for grassroots development. They are an intermediary between larger funders and popular groups. Strong NGOs help create and maintain the autonomy and the learning space for grassroots development. BRAC and the Grameen Bank in Bangladesh and many others, are democratically structured, informed from below, and strong enough to negotiate with government and international agencies on behalf of grassroots groups.

Storage, Marketing and Trade. Village-based grain *banks* (in Africa, a precolonial food security feature which nearly collapsed during the colonial era) are being revived in the Sahel and Zimbabwe. The grain banks provide rural people with local communal storage for grains. The local storage permits communities to offer higher prices to producers and lower prices to consumers than urban-based or controlled marketing and storage systems. The grain banks also allow local communities to trade among themselves, to balance out local shortfalls with local (and stored) surpluses. [21]

Also in Zimbabwe, farmers' associations—two-thirds of whose members are women—provide an organized way to share labor and purchase and sell in bulk, thereby assuring cost savings and higher prices for producers. These associations are self-managed by farmers and have demonstrated their value to rural households by supporting greater food retention by households, and higher household incomes from crop sales, as compared to households not involved in associations.[22]

Community Action. Community action promotes local survival and integrity and can alert astute and sensitive decision makers to the reactions to policy and program outcomes. Local people most affected by environmental change have taken the lead in protesting natural resources abuses for commercial purposes, and in offering alternatives that reflect their needs and resources rather than the wants (often of a luxury nature) of outsiders. Much attention has been given to the Chipko movement in India, which has protested outside commercial exploitation of forests by hugging trees. Women have played a major role in Chipko, especially in organizing and showing the economic value of forests and woodlands. Reforestation and local political organizing have become features of the movement.

Sustainability. In many parts of the South, survival is the first order of business, particularly, survival of the most vulnerable groups in the society. Many of these groups have demonstrated the strength and adaptability of their coping mechanisms. These survival skills have often been an unspoken rationale for officials ignoring cases of need, and for the introduction of severe austerity measures as part of World Bank financed structural adjustment programs.[23] On the other hand, local communities have used these skills to sustain the integrity of their societies. During famine, for example, consumption of household seed supplies is one of the last survival strategies people adopt.

Sustainability relates to production systems that do not deplete the natural resource base to the point where survival is impossible. In the alternative economy, the shift is from survival to long-term sustainability.

Environmental Integrity. Contrary to popular assumptions, farmers do not indiscriminately destroy their natural resource base. Rural communities have shown a strong sensitivity to sustaining the environment for continued use. Soil fertility is maintained through sensitive farming practices (intercropping, rotation, fertilization); erosion is controlled through intercropping, and terraces have been an important feature of local systems (often deteriorated in recent years) in the Philippines, Peru, Tanzania and other countries; and tree and grass cover is preserved and regularly utilized. As already mentioned, the integration of wild with domestic plants continues the genetic diversity of the environment.

In Niger, common labor is withheld from farmers using tractors, not as a Luddite reaction, but as a way to protect the soil cover and provide adequate land for all. The farmers realize that the deeper ploughing achieved with mechanical ploughing reduces soil fertility and increases the likelihood of erosion, while increasing the demand on the available land because tractor farmers must open new plots of land as existing ones more readily wear out.[24]

Diversity. Sustainability also means maintaining a broad diversity of crops for local and external use. Top quality is not always defined as the prettiest looking fruit, but refers also to the storage life of a product, the variety of uses to which that crop can be put, and the ease with which that crop can be raised without the application of expensive inputs. It reflects the capacity of the local community to produce and multiply the seed material needed each crop season, and the calculation of economic profitability based on the intellectual property contributed by local farmers in seed selection, use of appropriate farm practices, and market price.

Local community organizations contribute to diversity by recognizing, encouraging and using locally developed techniques and materials in their production systems. For example, in most low income communities, informal businesses regularly recycle materials, thereby adding new value to numerous products which would be considered garbage in many industrialized countries. Official support can facilitate those initiatives. In Eritrea, war and national policy have stimulated numerous programs of local production, and food security needs have given rise to a well-organized food distribution system under the local control.[25]

Equity. Equity incorporates leveling wealth, easy access to decent jobs with adequate wages, and availability of social services that enhance people's lives. Equity involves restructuring production programs in agriculture to address local food needs, and ensuring that agricultural services, industry, manufacturing, trade, etc. provide value to producers while also meeting local consumer needs and sustaining the environment. Equity in a food security framework does not preclude exports. It does not imply a closed economic system, but places community priorities before external ones.

In an alternative economy, equity will address the need for women to acquire and use land for their own purposes, ensure that landless households receive decent wages for their labor, and open up opportunities for the landless to acquire and/or use land for their own needs. An emphasis on equity will assure that agricultural prices provide a return to farmers that allows them to work their land in careful and sustaining ways. In addition, equity means that agriculture as well as industry, tourism and other urban-centered sectors will be served by research, transportation, storage, marketing, energy and credit.

Next Steps

An important reason for the perpetuation of the prevailing export driven, green revolution agricultural system is the effectiveness with which it has been billed a success. That success has been defined according to quantifiable and monetized economic criteria that exclude consideration of the human and environmental implications of production and growth. The criteria used are limited to such items as yield per acre, volume of fertilizer applied, number of farm machines in use, the contribution to export earnings and the like.

Markedly different conclusions would more than likely be drawn about the successes of modern agriculture if, in addition to these criteria, others were used. Such criteria could include: overall yield per farm unit; size of household garden; range of crops grown; extent of preservation and processing of local crops; use of farm materials to meet other home needs such as fuel, furniture and medicines; linkage between agriculture and other sectors; domestic food security; incidence of malnutrition and related diseases in rural areas; and the loss of soil fertility and pollution of ground and coastal water systems.

In building this alternative approach, one of the first and most significant challenges facing us is that of finding ways to work with local populations. We need to apply the knowledge and expertise evident in the development efforts cited earlier in order to shape the programs, policies and research that would contribute to the transformation of agriculture, other sectors of the economy, and the society at large.

As we approach this challenge of transformation, we must remind ourselves of a few development dilemmas:
- how are people to become productive if they are unhealthy?
- how are people to produce if they don't have access to resources?

- how are people to consume if they don't earn?
- how are people to earn if the markets and prices for their goods are unfavorable?
- how are people to conserve and enhance the environment if they are starving?
- how are people to become less dependent on handouts if their self-confidence, creativity and dignity are eroded?
- how are people to develop new approaches to production if powerful forces (local and international) enforce a standard top down approach?
- how is democracy to be built, if not from the bottom up?

Shaping the Alternative at the Local Level

At the level of the farm this would mean taking steps to reduce the heavy use of chemical fertilizers and pesticides by reintroducing crops into the farm plan that require fewer nutrients, and which, by virtue of their capacity to convert atmospheric nitrogen into a form that is usable by plants, can sustain economic yields with less need for added chemical nutrients. This technique of intercropping is traditional among small farmers in many countries, which means that local producers can be much more involved in the design and implementation of the farm plan than is the case with cropping systems that depend on introduced hybrid varieties. Intercropping is also a good example of a sustainable practice because it helps reduce the risk of damage from insects and disease by presenting the pathogens with a variety of host plants, some of which are not likely to be susceptible to the pest or disease. This technique also addresses the issue of reducing the farmer's economic risk by spreading farm income over a variety of crops capable of surviving a range of weather, soil and market conditions.

Crop rotation is another sustainable farming technique that is a proven method for resting soils and maintaining fertility over long periods. Fallowing of land and turning under the unused portion of a legume crop will improve soil structure and drainage while also reducing the extent of soil erosion. Maintaining a soil cover crop like sweet potatoes in between a crop of plantain also helps provide weed control, thereby reducing the need for cutlassing or herbicides. In addition, the staggered availability of the two crops spreads the cost of field management over a longer time period and over two crops instead of one, which enhances the cost effectiveness of the farm system and reduces the vulnerability of the farmer to the vagaries of weather, topography, market and imported technology.

Reshaping Services in Support of Sustainable Agriculture

An important aspect of the alternative is to reorient the approach to servicing the sector. In the area of research and technology, the key is to work with farmers in order to identify the more pressing problems affecting viable cropping systems, and to involve the farmers in the research exercise.

Changing the focus could mean that instead of conducting trials designed to test new fertilizers and chemicals, the research seeks to identify local varieties of crops that have been able to yield satisfactorily with little or no application of chemical fertilizer and to encourage farmers to select the seed material from those plants. By planting out these selected seeds, preferably on the farmer's plot, not only is local knowledge legitimized, but the care and eventual dissemination of the best varieties benefit from the vested ownership of farmers in a new piece of technology. It is well established that other farmers tend to accept ideas and methods much more readily when these are known to have been proven under conditions of weather and management that they understand.[26] The role of the trained researcher in this new scheme of things is to combine scientific knowledge with the local knowledge in order to test these techniques under a variety of conditions. They can then be presented in packages that are appropriately responsive to a wider range of farmers.

Once a suitable variety of local crop has been selected, seed multiplication is the next phase of support to farming and can also involve local farmers. One of the high cost items in modern agriculture is the seasonal purchase of the hybrid seed now being widely used. The conversion of part of a farm to seed multiplication allows for crop and income diversification, brings the supply line for seed much closer to the other farmers needing to replant, and allows for early observation of any deterioration of the variety under local conditions, an advantage that is completely lost when all seed material is imported.

Credit is another vital service that would be transformed in a sustainable agricultural system. Traditional credit schemes are often linked to the purchase of fertilizer and other imported inputs that are part of the modern package of production technology. In a sustainable system, credit would need to be guided by criteria that, for example, reward farmers for employing intercropping, rotation, integrated pest management and other such renewable husbandry methods. Production systems that employ these methods reduce the need for credit to buy chemicals and allow credit to be applied to other areas that have been neglected in the past. These include transportation and roads, marketing, agro-processing and training.

Integrating Farm Production

A major feature of modern agriculture is that the farm becomes dependent upon outside sources for the inputs necessary for production, and for the disposal of the goods produced. The result is extreme vulnerability to fluctuations in costs, prices, transport and distribution, and to the other systems essential to the operation of the farm. Segments of the economy dependent upon the farm sector are likewise vulnerable. A system of sustainable agriculture reduces the vulnerability of the farm sector to external forces, affecting both the input and the output phases of production.

Through the use of composting, for example, farmers ensure the recycling of farm materials into organic soil ameliorators and plant food. Traditional farm systems have employed this system of waste recycling for centuries and have managed to obtain satisfactory yields while improving soil structure, drainage and fertility, thus reducing soil erosion as a result of the increased levels of organic matter added to the land.

In addition to employing systems of on-farm composting to produce fertilizer, sustainable farming also utilizes the production of special green manure crops, preferably legumes for their nitrogen-fixing potential, which are turned into the soil as a means of directly improving texture and fertility and reducing the need to purchase chemical fertilizers.

Apart from the direct ecological and husbandry benefits resulting from diversifying the farm operation in order to produce inputs that would normally have to be purchased, this transformation of the input side of production can be matched with corresponding changes on the output side. By utilizing excess plant material, pen manure and other recyclable waste from the farm household in a biogas digester, a farm operation can generate much of the power needed to operate electric machinery, provide lights to the home and chicken house, and power a water pump for irrigation.

This integrated farm system reduces the need to import or otherwise purchase production inputs and diversifies the farm operation to allow energy, which also would have to be purchased, to be produced with materials available on the farm. In addition to the savings that can result, these innovations and the "new" skills required to operate such an integrated system are likely to create more jobs on the farm, and to be sufficiently challenging to the young rural person to reverse the drift to urban centers.

Making Links Between Sectors

A sustainable approach to agriculture also establishes links with other sectors. Once a transformation of farm production results in the availability of a wider variety of crops, marketing systems that have been established for a narrow range of chemically produced crops will need to be adjusted to handle new products. Hotel and restaurant operators who may have complained about a lack of variety in the locally available crops would now have access to a wider range of fruits, herbs, spices and vegetables. Agro-industries formerly dependent upon imported raw materials would have several types of local raw materials to choose from.

On the input side, sustainable agriculture requires a different training approach from researchers and extension agents who work with farmers. The quick and easy recommendation of toxic chemicals to take care of a pest or disease problem would need to be replaced by a more integrated knowledge of farming systems, an understanding of the interaction between the soil, plant and animal systems on the farm, and the capacity to work with farmers to devise viable and sustainable practices. The practice of training highly skilled specialists who have little knowledge of other disciplines, will need to change.

Alternative Trading

This is one of the most critical off-farm operations affecting the transition to a sustainable approach to agriculture. Postharvest handling, grading, storage, transportation, distribution and sale of farm products have become highly specialized fields that are controlled by institutions and persons who are often far removed from the farmer and the farm. In such circumstances, the farmer remains at the mercy of the forces of the free market. The impact of price fluctuations on the cacao, coffee and sugarcane producers of the South is well known.[27]

A sustainable approach to agriculture would address this relationship of the farmer to the marketplace by ensuring that more of the operations of grading, packaging and transporting involve the farmer and other rural dwellers. This would mean, for example, the construction of appropriate packing and handling facilities in areas that are accessible to the farmer and rural workers, providing training to the workers who will now operate these packing facilities. This ensures that as new jobs are created by an increasingly diversified agriculture, the people in the rural areas are also the beneficiaries.

To actively promote this alternative trading arrangement, policies to improve internal and external food marketing should be in place to avoid duplicating the situation where all incentives and infrastructure are provided for export marketing, while local food shortages persist. This would mean price and tax policies that provide an incentive to producers targeting the local market, and appropriate import pricing that allows locally produced items to remain competitively priced.

Policies and programs are needed to facilitate improvements in the forecasting of local food shortages and surpluses, monitor local and international prices, match agrometeorology data with market conditions, and develop systems capable of accurately predicting the crop supply situation.[28] These measures would facilitate the establishment of a comprehensive production and trading system responsive to both domestic and external needs.

Shaping the Alternative at the Regional and International Levels

The small size of developing countries, the fragility of their environment, an economic openness and vulnerability to external market forces, mounting debt and debt service obligations, and rising food deficits are among the long list of pressing problems underscoring the need for a regional approach to development. To be meaningful to the local population, however, regional cooperation has to translate into practical measures which, in the case of agriculture, expand the possibilities for food production, increase the use of locally grown food, link industry more closely with agriculture, and develop the promotional, marketing and transportation capabilities of the regional economy.

An alternative regional agenda would also depend heavily on the active participation of the people of the region. Their knowledge of the local situation must help shape the policies and programs aimed at increasing the output of goods and services, ensuring improvements in individual and household incomes and enhancing the natural resource base fundamental to sustaining any process of growth. This would mean the initiation of a genuine process of democratic development that requires direct, community level involvement in the planning and decision-making process.

As we look to a future where trading blocs of large industrialized nations increasingly dominate the world economy, our definition of "region" needs to be broadened to include countries previously excluded from attempts at cooperation. In the Caribbean, for example, countries like Haiti, Cuba, and the Dominican Republic must now be viewed as full and active partners in the process of regional development. Regional and subregional initiatives that are already under way will need to expand to take this into account.

Vacillation on the question of regional unity needs to be replaced by a firm resolve at all levels to put aside petty biases and unfounded fears about what constitutes the Horn Region, East Africa, the Pacific or the Caribbean. This also means putting to rest once and for all the notion that the answer to the problems of poverty and underdevelopment lie in adopting the systems of production and governance that others have fashioned according to their local conditions. The alternative development approach that we have discussed here is based on the notion that it is communities of farmers, women, technicians, workers, policymakers and others who must accept the responsibility for fashioning their own future.

People in the South who embark upon this new and different approach to development will interact with an international community where most aid donors and trading partners remain committed to the trickle-down, export led model of economic growth. This means that international policies and programs remain unsupportive of a development agenda that would have women, food, jobs, health services, the environment, regional cooperation and unity as priorities.

In the area of foreign assistance, our interaction with the international community must seek support that helps us through a period of transition from a near total dependence on exports to a greater reliance on our local and regional markets. We would require assistance to convert our use of land to a cropping pattern that would allow us to feed our people, to process our raw materials, and make links among all sectors of our emerging regional economy.

In the area of trade, we need agreements that enable us to sell goods manufactured with local materials by local firms employing local workers under the same rights and working conditions that are guaranteed by the International Labor Organization (ILO) and other relevant international conventions. We need commitments from our international nongovernmental organization (NGO) partners that our efforts to promote trade among ourselves and other forms of self-reliance will be supported, and that efforts to undermine regional cooperation in the name of trade liberalization (as is currently being attempted at the Uruguay Round of the General Agreement on Tariffs and Trade (GATT) talks), will be condemned.

Clearly what we are presenting here is a new model of balanced economic growth: an approach that reduces our dependence on production for export, particularly those exports that do not generate linkages to the rest of the local and regional economy. We are also talking about an approach that reduces our dependence on imports of technology, raw materials and expertise. Instead, we are advocating an approach to development that is based more on our own realities, experiences, and expertise. We are advocating greater opportunities for building self-reliance, and for practicing effective participation in the decisions affecting our lives. We are insisting on an approach to development that is self-sustaining, equitable and participatory, and is linked to other cultures and economies in ways that violate neither the dignity of our workers and farmers nor the integrity and beauty of our environment.

Concluding Comments

Reshaping an economy is an extremely complex task, and entails raising public awareness, embarking on rigorous reflection and research into alternative production systems to redress the failings of current modes of economic analysis, building leadership that can undertake the transition process, and encouraging political change. This paper has attempted to highlight existing practices that meet the criteria for a participatory, self-reliant, equitable and sustainable approach to agriculture as one of the many aspects of transformation needed in countries impoverished by the trickle-down, free market model of economic growth.

The dimensions of the challenge of an alternative approach to development are so mind-boggling that many seek the path of least resistance, accepting quick fix, one-stop solutions which are no solutions at all. Fortunately, more and more, people at the grassroots are understanding why current models of growth have failed. These models, whether they were driven by the greed of the marketplace or by the power of the central plan, failed because they were designed by elites in the North in collaboration with elites in the South and do not correspond to local conditions. These strategies failed because they assumed that poverty could be overcome by outsiders, without consultation and partnership with the people who experience that poverty. They failed because growth in the South was linked to the needs and demands of the North, and ignored the needs and demands of the people of the South.

Today there are many other forces at work, aimed at building an alternative development movement centered on the efforts of people working at the local level to fashion a more equitable, sustainable and participatory approach to development. Until recently, this important work was constrained by the small number of persons working towards the same goal at local, national, regional and international levels. Not many NGOs grappled with the task of translating the vision of grassroots development into a model that blended food sufficiency, health care, affordable housing, popular education, and local knowledge with the broader issues of world trade, global environment, international debt, foreign aid, gender, and the rights of workers, indigenous peoples, and landless people. Today, widespread poverty, famine, war, and environmental destruction provide us with irrefutable evidence of the failure of the two major economic paradigms to resolve the problems of the majority of Earth's inhabitants. In the face of these global disasters the challenge for those of us who dare to change things is unambiguous.

It is no longer sufficient to analyze and advocate for change; it is no longer sufficient to design, fund and carry out successful development projects. Now it is essential that those of us who accept the challenge of working for a safe, just and sustainable world make changes in our personal and institutional lifestyles so that we hear and listen to the voices of the poor, and find the courage and humility to enter into partnerships with those for whom the marketplace has never held any magic.

In closing, let us remind ourselves of several important questions that require further attention, research, analysis and debate as the local community moves toward transforming its own economy.

- What are the traditional and new forms of consultation that would allow for broad-based participation in decision making in a timely and effective way?
- What are the implications for existing forms of parliamentary democracy, laws and constitutions?

- What mechanisms of accountability exist that allow leadership to be held responsive to agreed goals? How does this work?
- How are the "new issues" of job security, health and safety, equity, and ecological responsibility factored into decision making about growth sectors that are performing well, or which require more resources or less, etc?
- What new planning and management tools and skills are needed as these "new issues" get factored into the development equation?
- How are these applied in a development process that is still largely affected by institutions, thinking and practices that are driven by easily quantifiable benchmarks, such as gross national product (the total value of a nation's output of goods and services), output per hectare, number of jobs created, etc?
- What policy measures and practical incentives can be fashioned to make environmental care and enhancement worthwhile investments?
- Are incomes taxed to pay for those activities that are ecologically sound? Are violators of the ecology penalized and revenue from fines used to pay for investment in the environment?
- What lessons can we draw from debt swaps or other attempts at financing environmental enhancement?
- In the context of increasing unilateral global military action, and potential countervailing forces of large economic blocs, how are choices made that minimize military and economic intervention and disruption?
- What have we learned about the conduct of relations between states that can lay the basis for dialogue and discussion to replace unilateral action by more powerful states?
- What is the most effective role that NGOs can play and how can their activities be supported?
- What steps are needed to ensure linkage between sectors?
- How is regional cooperation among states affected by efforts at national level transformation?
- What are the implications for gender, race, class and political status?
- Where do the resources come from that will finance this transition?

Notes

1. James Robertson, *Future Wealth: A New Economics For the 21st Century* (New York: The Bootstrap Press, 1990), 1. Tom Robertson, "Physical, Economic, and Social Aspects of Development in the Eastern Caribbean" (Washington, D. C.: 1985), 5.
2. James Robertson, *Future Wealth*, 1.
3. James Robertson, *Future Wealth*, 1.
4. The Bank Information Center, ed., *Funding Ecological and Social Destruction: The World Bank and the International Monetary Fund* (Washington, D. C.: 1989), 1.
5. Vandana Shiva, *The Violence of the Green Revolution: Ecological Degradation and Political Conflict in the Punjab* (India: Vandana Shiva, 1989), 31.
6. Tony Hill, "Commodities and Third World Development" in *People's Economics: Report on a Third World Network Meeting* (Penang: Third World Network, 1990), 22.
7. Dennis Pantin, *Into the Valley of Debt: An Alternative to the IMF/World Bank Path* (Trinidad and Tobago: Gloria V. Ferguson Ltd., 1989), 18. James Robertson, *Future Wealth*, 1.
8. Third World Network, *Third World Development or Crisis?* (Penang: Third World Network, 1984), 78.
9. Shiva, *People's Economics*, 24.
10. International Movement for Ecological Agriculture, in *Global Crisis Towards Ecological Agriculture* (Penang: Third World Network, 1990).
11. The Bank Information Center, *Funding Ecological and Social Destruction*, 1.
12. Bread for the World, Institute on Hunger and Development, *Hunger 1990: A Report On The State of World Hunger* (Washington, D. C.: Institute on Hunger and Development, Bread for the World, 1990), 6.
13. The Bank Information Center, *Funding Ecological and Social Destruction*, 5.
14. Lori Ann Thrupp, "Legitimizing Local Knowledge: From Displacement to Empowerment for Third World People," *Agriculture and Human Values* (1989): 13. *Report: The International Conference on Popular Participation in the Recovery and Development Process in Africa* (Arusha: Iowa State University, 1990).
15. Roland Bunch, *Two Ears of Corn* (Oklahoma: World Neighbors, 1982), 38.
16. Bunch, *Two Ears*, 38.
17. Roland Bunch, *Report of the Plant Genetics Resources Center, Ethiopia: Ten Years of Collection, Conservation, Utilization 1976–1986* (Addis Ababa: The Plant Genetics Resources Center, 1986).
18. Bill Rau, conversations in 1989.
19. Gabriela National Center, *Empowering Women in a Situation of Crisis* (Philippines: Gabriela, 1989), 36.
20. Rau, conversations in 1990.
21. Rau, conversations in 1990.
22. National Farmers Association of Zimbabwe, *Progress Report Five Years on 1980–1986* (Harare: 1986).

23. The Bank Information Center, *Funding Ecological and Social Destruction*, 1.
24. Rau, conversations in 1990.
25. James Fierbrace with Stuart Holland, *Never Kneel Down* (Trenton, N.J.: The Red Sea Press, 1985), 70.
26. Roland Bunch, *Low Input Restoration in Honduras: Cantarranas Farmer-to-Farmer Extension Programme* (London: International Institute for Environment and Development, 1990), 8.
27. Tony Hill, *Peoples Economics;* The Bank Information Center, *Funding Ecological and Social Destruction*, 1.
28. Tom Robertson, *"Physical, Economic and Social Aspects,"* 17.

CHAPTER THREE

RESOURCE WARS
Nation-State Conflicts of the 20th Century

Jason W. Clay

Jason Clay, director of research at the Boston-based human rights group, Cultural Survival, and past editor of the agency's highly acclaimed quarterly, gives a sobering account of the politics of famine and devastating toll of rising militarism and regional conflicts on world hunger and environmental degradation. He does this in the context of ongoing struggles between modern states and the"nations" of people groups found therein. His prognosis—a further disintegration of states as seen this year in the former Soviet Union and the Horn of Africa—is doubtless prescient if not hopeful, and serves as an important reminder to nongovernmental organizations to do prodigious homework on how their interventions may relate to specific people groups and their resource base within states. On the brighter side, Clay cites encouraging examples of indigenous peoples who have managed to turn traditional skills to modern livelihoods on their own terms.

THE BERLIN WALL IS NOT the only thing that has crumbled in Europe. Our basic assumptions about the role of the state, which appeared to be written in stone until only a couple of years ago, are crumbling as well. The rise of nationalism and recent moves toward democratic pluralism and autonomy in Eastern Europe, the USSR, Africa and Southeast Asia demonstrate that seemingly unchangeable systems of government can crumble almost overnight. Cultural identity, more than ideology, appears to be the building block for truly democratic, bottom-up political systems.

Today's nations are challenging age-old notions that states are the basic building blocks for global peace and environmental security.

At stake is not the existence, or even legitimacy, of states, but rather the survival of nations, which involves such issues as local control of the land and resources, cultural freedom, and the political autonomy necessary to ensure survival. Indeed, nations' food security and ecological equilibrium have never been more at risk than amid twentieth-century proliferation of weapons, development programs, and state appropriation of resources.

Nations and States

There are today about 170 states in the world, up from the 50 or so at the time of World War II, but considerably fewer than the more than 200 that will likely exist by the year 2000. These states encompass approximately 5,000 nations. Even though it may feel to most of us like states have existed forever, the majority have been created since World War II. By contrast, most nations—generally characterized by distinct language, culture and history, territorial bases and self-government that predates the creation of modern states—have been around for hundreds of years, in some cases even millennia.

Most nation peoples believe that states have only as much legitimacy as is bestowed voluntarily by those incorporated into the state political system. This will take some time. Oromos in Ethiopia do not think of themselves as Ethiopians, Kayapo in Brazil do not think of themselves first or even foremost as Brazilians, and the Penan of Sarawak, Malaysia barely even know what Malaysia is much less think of themselves as part of that country. This is not uncommon; states mean very little, at least in a positive sense, to most nation peoples. For example, there are more than 130 nations in the USSR, 180 in Brazil, 450 in Nigeria, 350 in India, 450 in Indonesia, 300 in the Cameroon and some 80 in Ethiopia.

Very simply put, there is no such thing as a "nation state." All states contain more than one nation, try as many of them might to eliminate or assimilate ("melt") them. Every state is multinational; or put another way, every contemporary state is an empire. Furthermore, modern states, particularly Third World states, are ruled like empires, that is, from the top down. This situation is leading many nations to ask what costs and what benefits they get from their incorporation into states. As a result of such analyses, the rise of nationalism should surprise no one.

The refusal of states to acknowledge their cultural diversity is not only one of the major causes of the rise of nationalism and "ethnic" conflict throughout the world; it has, more importantly, caused the loss of more information about the Earth's resources and how they can be managed sustainably than has any other single factor. The knowledge of a single nation about resource management, gathered over centuries, cannot be duplicated by hundreds of person years of research by scores of scientists.

Imagine, then, the impact on humanity of the loss of nations. During this, the century of progress, civilization and enlightenment, there is good evidence that more nations have disappeared than during any previous one in history. Brazil, for example, has "lost" one Indian nation per year since the turn of the century while government officials and planners have done their best to "develop" the Amazon into a wasteland.

To put it another way, nations are disappearing at a faster rate than the often fragile resource bases that they have used, and yet maintained, over the centuries. Even though our generation has the most enlightened international laws, treaties and conventions on human rights and genocide, we have, arguably, the most violations as well. At the heart of this apparent contradiction is the state building, nation destroying process. Simply put, states cannot get at the resources (for example, land, trees, minerals, water) without denying the rights of the indigenous inhabitants, the nations that have lived in and maintained the resource base.

Nations and Development

It is only now, however, that scientists have begun to take interest in the sustainable resource management systems of nation peoples. In most cases, these systems modify the traditional resource base by intensifying the occurrence of the useful species but nonetheless retaining a wide range of useful species and most of the genetic resource base. Sustainable resource management does not mean the retention of every species (that is, preservation) but rather the wise use of a resource base which allows most species to exist (that is, conservation) and reduces the risk of nations becoming dependent upon a single resource. Many scientists would argue, for example, that there are not ten square kilometers of rainforest anywhere in the world that have not been modified by people.

There are about 600 million nation peoples who retain a strong social and cultural identity as well as an attachment to a specific territory. Nations are distinguished from ethnic groups who, though much larger in absolute numbers, have usually made an accommodation with states by trading away political autonomy for the ability to retain and practice other cultural beliefs. Recent protests in Eastern Europe and the USSR have shown that ethnic groups, however, can push for autonomy, even to the point of asserting national claims for independence. In short, ethnic groups can become nations. Israel is a prime example.

Nations account for 10 to 15 percent of the world's population but have traditional claims to 25 to 30 percent of the earth's surface area and resources. This is one of the major reasons for conflict between nations and states. Decimated through contact and colonization from 1500 to 1900, the world's nation peoples have increased in size tremendously since 1900 and especially since World War II, precisely when most states have been created. Thus states are established exactly when many nations feel that it is possible to push for more autonomy and regain the political independence that had been increasingly denied them under colonialism.

Nations have had many different experiences in their incorporation into states, particularly in the postcolonial period. Some nations, like the Kikuyu in Kenya, decided to take their chances in the new states, becoming, if you will, ethnic groups by choice. Other groups, like the Mbundu in Angola, knew that they had no chance of gaining power within the new state, so they took up arms immediately. Still other nations like the numerous isolated Indian nations in the Amazon were so untouched that they were not aware of the political significance of decolonization. Finally, some nations, such as a dozen or so groups in Burma, negotiated local autonomy as an overall condition of postcolonial independence only to see it taken away by military coups sponsored by dominant groups. Each of these situations can, and often has, prompted numerous groups around the world to take up arms.

Since World War II, many factors have affected negatively the willingness of nations to accept the *a priori* legitimacy of states. In most instances "nation states" have been created in the image of and are dominated by only one or a few of the nations in each state. When cooperation between nations breaks down, dictatorships and one party states become the norm. Sub-Saharan Africa is a perfect example of the problem.

The elites who dominate new states, particularly in the Third World, can be characterized by a winner-take-all mentality. Those who control states make laws in their own image and in their own interest. They control foreign investment and assistance (both development and military), which are used to reinforce the power of those who rule. They also usually fix local commodity prices and control exports. These sources of income account for two-thirds of state revenues. The final third of state revenues are derived from taxes, often disproportionately levied on nation peoples. Thus, government is the biggest game in town.

Those who rule decide the national laws (including who owns which resources and which traditional resource tenure systems will be honored by the state) and often religion, language, cultural traditions and holidays. Because they are integral to the survival of nations, it is these issues that often trigger violent confrontation.

Nations and Natural Resources

Since World War II, there has been a growing awareness of the finite nature of the Earth's resources. This has led to the state invasion of remote nation areas and the appropriation of resources (for example, Indian land throughout the Amazon, pastoralists' land throughout Africa, oil from the Kurds in Iraq, timber from the Penan of Malaysia). Profits from the sale of such resources accrue to those who control the state. Those who can control and sell such resources will gain considerably. Thus, traditional resource rights of nations that may have been constitutionally guaranteed as a condition of independence are often subsequently denied. This, too, understandably leads to conflict.

While I am focusing mostly on the relationship of Third World states to nations, it must be noted that so-called developed countries are not unwitting observers but rather active participants in the creation of the international state/trading system. The West created most Third World states in order to maintain global stability, to facilitate free trade, and to reduce the costs of governing far-flung empires. Our investments, political interference, and foreign and military assistance have helped to maintain the dictatorships and single-party states that dominate the world today, and provide the free flow of resources needed by multinational corporations to feed our voracious appetite for consumer goods.

Still, the Third World political reality is that, with or without our assistance (but usually with it), nation groups that resist the authority of the state are destroyed. It is no accident that more nation groups have been destroyed in the twentieth century than during any century in history, because it is only recently that we have had the technology that has allowed us to inventory and exploit the world's resources.

Some larger nations can physically defend their groups and their resources from state invasion or at least hamper significantly the invasion of their areas. Smaller nations, however, can rarely physically defend their homelands from invasion. If the rights of these groups are to be protected, they must be defended at the level of the state or multilateral organizations. But here lies another contradiction: are states or multilateral state organizations genuinely interested in the survival of nations, or would they rather see them quietly disappear?

Of the world's 5,000 nations, perhaps 500 could physically defend themselves in armed conflict. It is these groups that have taken up arms in the past two decades as they have seen their political and cultural autonomy as well as their resource base curtailed. Of the 120 or so shooting wars today, 75 percent are between nations and the states who claim them as citizens. These are the conflicts that many analysts refer to as low-intensity conflicts.

What do such low-intensity, nation/state conflicts produce? Most of the victims of such conflicts are women, children and the elderly. Since World War II, at least 5 million people have been killed as a result of such conflicts; even larger numbers have died as a result of malnutrition and famine. While some 15 million have officially fled across international borders as refugees (with maybe that many more going unnoticed), more than 150 million others have been forced to flee their homelands and become internally displaced. Most of this displacement has occurred in the name of "national" integration, development, or the appropriation of resources for the benefit of all.

Displaced nation people, whether they cross international boundaries or not, cause environmental degradation and conflict with local groups. For example, the 1984–86 government sponsored resettlement program in Ethiopia during the recent famine led to the clearing of 8 percent of Ethiopia's remaining forests in 1985 alone. Displaced nation people also suffer from malnutrition, disease and poverty. Ironically, most displacement results from bilateral and multilaterally funded development programs that displace those groups who are powerless to oppose it.

No state ideology seems to protect nations or to promote pluralism better than any other. States, of both the left and right, as well as religious and sectarian states, deny the rights of nations. Those who control states see nations as a threat to "national" security. They justify even the forced assimilation of nation peoples in the name of progress.

So what are the products of nation/state conflicts? Nearly half of all Third World debt is for weapons purchases that are used to engage in armed conflict with nation peoples who are supposedly already citizens of the state. Military expenditures are greater than all social and development programs combined. For example, it was estimated that in 1988 states spent an average of $25,000 per soldier and less than $350 per student. Foreign debts (caused by military expenditures and the capital flight of elites) led to austerity measures and provided the rationale for the further appropriation of the land and resources of nations. It should be noted in passing that Third World elites have foreign assets equal to the entire Third World debt. Thus, while everyone is responsible for paying such debts, only some benefited from the original loans.

In short, then, the appropriation of nation resources leads to conflict, which leads to weapons purchases, which leads to debt, which leads to the need to appropriate more resources. Thus, there is a spiralling escalation of the conflict with no end in sight.

State control of nation people is seen as essential to state survival, yet the measures taken fuel nation hostility, making control imperative. This is clearly a case where the cure is worse than the disease. State programs such as relocation, colonization, resettlement and actually forcing peasantry into artificial villages ensure nation control by states as well as the control of nation lands and resources. Food and famine become weapons in nation/state conflict. Displacement, malnutrition, environmental degradation, refugees and genocide become commonplace.

The bottom line is that state control of nations and the dismantling of nation sociopolitical organizations, usually through multilaterally or bilaterally funded development programs, but also through famine relief and militarization programs, creates dependent populations from formerly self-sufficient ones. Thus already heavily indebted, Third World states are faced with populations that can only look to the state for basic ties. However, since such groups are already systematically discriminated against, they receive little or no help.

Indigenous Knowledge and Resource Rights

In the recent rush to discover, inventory and save the world's biodiversity, there is considerable prospecting being done by corporations, scientists, NGOs and governments. This is probably the last great resource grab of the twentieth century. In the name of saving the world, or at least salvaging information before it disappears, shamans, tribes and groups of people are being ripped off without a second thought. Basic agreements that would be signed with any Western researcher (contracts, licensing payments or royalties) for information, are routinely denied to groups that provide culturally specific discoveries that have taken generations, even millennia, to test and develop.

This is not to say that indigenous peoples should have all the rights to genetic or biodiversity materials or even necessarily to medicines and cures that they have discovered and developed, but rather that they, too, have rights just as do scientists, countries and corporations. Without the cooperation of all these players, few raw materials would end up as new products. However, indigenous peoples are unique in this list, because they are without exception excluded from profiting from their information.

Nations and Resource Management

There are many who now argue that nation people degrade their own resource bases, often fragile ecosystems, and that the world cannot stand by and allow this to happen. The next cure for a disease, it is argued, could be going up in smoke in the rainforest. (It doesn't take a rocket scientist to look at our own backyard and ask what right we have to tell anyone how to manage their resources!) This whole issue requires some discussion, because it is often couched in the language of the greatest good for the greatest number. In fact, the situation is almost always the reverse. It is the goods for only a few people who have political or consumer power.

What then is the record of nation peoples as conservationists? Do they merely use resources or do they manage them? Anthropologists, who have done the most research on economic activities of nation peoples, frequently err on the side of romanticism in their views of such peoples as "the once and future resource managers." In fact, nation peoples track records are extremely mixed. Yet, many practices are indeed conservationist even though their "scientific" basis may not yet be understood. It should be noted, too, that nation peoples have domesticated most of our basic foods (60 percent coming from the new world alone). Field trials of new crops and management systems continue. It is doubtful that researchers or scientists conduct even 5 percent of the field trials. The rest is done by nation peoples and peasant farmers trying to find a better way to make a living.

Nation peoples, because of the romantic views concerning their cultural heritage, are often forced to adhere to a different standard than everyone else. Yet over the centuries it is clear that their resource management systems, unlike our own, are in a relatively sustainable statis with the environment. Through the centuries, nation peoples throughout the world have developed sustained-yield subsistence systems which often combine root crops, vegetable crops and select tree crops that, in turn, improve hunting, fishing and gathering. Domesticated animals and cash or marketable crops have been added to the mix.

The various world views and beliefs about the environment that distinguish nation peoples from us as well as from each other lead to culturally specific systems of resource management. These systems are rarely random or opportunistic. Nation peoples are not preservationists in the sense that they are actively involved in manipulating their environment. Instead, they are conservationists because they know that they must use their resources but leave enough to guarantee the survival of future generations. Some of their systems are sustainable over time, others are not. Some are sustainable under certain conditions but become destructive under others. Some individuals are more cautious and conserving of resources than others in the same group.

Yet nation peoples are becoming extinct at an even faster rate than the regions they have traditionally inhabited. For example, one indigenous group per year has disappeared in Brazil since 1900, a third of all the cultures. In the same time about 10 percent of the Amazon has been lost. Human rights violations precede environmental degradation.

Not all the extinction is overtly violent. In many societies undergoing rapid change, young people no longer want to learn the methods by which their ancestors maintained fragile regions. Little time remains if this information is to be maintained for future generations.

Resource management systems of nation peoples stress sophisticated and extensive knowledge of the local environment. They are based on the view that the environment is the source of life for further generations and should therefore not be pillaged for short-term gain and long-term loss. Unlike farmers in mid-latitude areas who depend on machinery, specialized seeds, fertilizers and pesticides and who may view the land as their adversary, nation people see the land and other resources as the lifeblood of their nations. Taking a quick look around the world, which systems leave more resources for future generations?

What conditions, then, encourage nation people living in fragile environments to conserve resources? The most important factors, it appears, are resource rights (for example, to land, timber, water), the ability to organize themselves to protect their land and resources base, and their ability to transform traditional resource management systems to meet their modern needs. It is in fact the adaptation of traditional resource management systems, rather than their wholesale abandonment in favor of more advanced agricultural technologies, that will allow nation peoples to develop more rational, long-term land use patterns. By contrast, development efforts of the post-World War II period have proven disastrous for nation peoples regardless of the size of the projects or technical inputs.

By discovering the extent to which traditional management practices can be altered, more cash crops can be generated to meet the increasing material demands of nation peoples. Very few traditional resource management schemes are in use and working today. Most traditional systems have been adapted to meet the increased material needs of the groups in question or the curtailment of their resource rights by the state. Some interesting adaptations are:

- The Huichol Indians of Mexico, instead of selling their timber to companies, are now harvesting it themselves, processing it and making products. In this way they earn 300 times more per log and reduce deforestation in their forests.
- The Irulu of India, recently pushed off their land, use their hunting and gathering skills to earn an income from snakes. They catch poisonous ones to milk for venom, and they use nonpoisonous ones to rid villages of rodents, which currently eat 10 to 15 percent of all grain harvested in the country.
- The Kuna Indians of Panama have established the first nation's biosphere in the world. They now earn income from ecotourism as well as from the fees they charge scientists to do research on their land.
- The Xavante of Brazil are learning how to process and sell traditional products. They have set up a trading company to export their produce to countries where the crops can fetch a higher price.
- The regional Indian organization of Cauca, Colombia, has established tree nurseries so that more than fifty communities are now able to reforest areas that they recently won back from cattle ranchers. The program has been so successful that colonists have started to plant trees as well.
- The Kung San of Namibia have reclaimed part of their traditional land in the Kalahari Desert. They have extended their economic base beyond traditional hunting and

gathering to include herding domesticated animals, gardening, and wage labor.

Nation peoples' very existence demonstrates their ability to maintain the earth's resources for centuries without destroying them. While respect for resources is not universal among native cultures, it is a common practice. Respect for resources, with some groups at least, reveals itself in such beliefs as the "sacredness" of the earth and the spiritual characteristics of aspects of the environment.

However, it must be remembered in passing that much of the pressure on nations' resource bases comes not from within but from the insatiable consumption patterns and nonsustainable resource utilization practices in industrialized countries. Whether nation peoples will be able to survive, often in fragile habitats, will depend in large part on our halting or reducing the practices in the industrialized regions of the world that threaten both the world's cultural and biological diversity.

The Shape of Things to Come

As the industrial powers begin to seriously reconsider the roots of their debts and adopt new policies for getting their own houses in order, they will also reduce their overall assistance to Third World states. In the past, most assistance has been for military (writ "internal, national security") purposes. Cutting these umbilical cords to elites who dominate Third World states will unleash changes similar to those that have taken place recently in the USSR and Eastern Europe. Unfortunately, it is highly unlikely that such transitions will be peaceful in the Third World.

In fact, as the United States, the USSR and Europe shift their focus to their own internal state structures and problems, existing regional conflicts will become increasingly violent. Furthermore, conflicts long thought to be dormant will be rekindled, either because of the repression fostered by foreign military assistance or because it will no longer be possible for elites to play foreign political interests off of one another.

Consequently, the number of shooting wars within states is likely to increase, precisely at a time when arms manufacturers and NATO and Warsaw pact countries are trying to dump obsolete weapons, and Third World arms producers are seeking to expand their own sales to subsidize their weapons needs and to earn much needed foreign exchange. Such conflicts will spawn huge numbers of refugees and displaced people, not to mention untold environmental degradation. These conflicts inevitably disrupt food production too, making "development" impossible. More importantly, children will become malnourished and the quality—even the very existence—of the education they so sorely need to help them face the next millennium will suffer. International law has not proven itself to hold an answer: we have more human rights covenants and treaties than ever before, and this century has seen more genocides than any other. It is ironic that the demilitarization of Soviet states and the United States will lead to a lot of weapons being dumped on the market at low prices, enough to fuel many Third World conflicts. It is also the case that as those sources of weapons appear to be drying up, the Third World countries will begin to manufacture their own and sell them to others as a way to subsidize development and production.

This is not a worst case, doomsday scenario. Considerable evidence points to an increase in internal regional conflicts in Africa, Asia and the Middle East during the 1990s. Even the 500th anniversary of the colonization of the Americas will bring into sharp contrast the different perspectives of the colonizers and the colonized.

The last decade of the millennium is upon us. It promises to be extremely important in the struggles between nations and states. Yet the struggles of nations for autonomy in the USSR and Eastern Europe give hope that the world's cultural diversity will survive well into the next millennium. States are too large to solve the small problems and too small to solve the large ones. Put another way, states are too big to feed people, but too small to conserve the numerous, interrelated fragile ecosystems that we all depend upon. Changes regarding the rights of nations, similar to what we have seen in former Eastern Bloc states, will have to take place in the United States and U.S.-allied block of states before the rights of nations to land and resources and the autonomy to exercise those rights will be guaranteed.

Additional Readings

Clay, Jason W. "Indigenous Peoples in the Modern World." *Development Forum* (January/February: 1989): 12–13.

———. "Latest Thinking: What's a Nation?" *Mother Jones* (October 1990): 28–30.

———. "Indigenous Peoples: The Miner's Canary for the Twentieth Century." In Suzanne Head and Robert Heinzman (eds.), *Lessons of the Rainforest*. San Francisco: Sierra Club Books, 1990.

For more information on the issues raised in this chapter, see the following theme issues of the journal Cultural Survival Quarterly:

"Deforestation: The Human Costs." 6 no. 2 (1982).

"Nomads—Stopped in Their Tracts?" 8 no. 1 (1984).

"Hunters and Gatherers." 8 no. 3 (1984).

"Organizing to Survive." 8 no. 4 (1984).

"Nation, Tribe and Ethnic Group in Africa." 9 no. 3 (1985).

"Multilateral Banks and Indigenous Peoples." 10 no. 1 (1986).

"Grassroots Economic Development." 11 no. 1 (1987).

"Militarization and Indigenous Peoples." 11 no. 3–4 (1987).

"Resettlement and Relocation." 12 no. 3–4 (1988).

"Land and Resources: The Finite Frontier." 14 no. 4 (1990).

"Intellectual Property Rights: The Politics of Ownership." 15 no. 3 (1991).

CHAPTER FOUR

FOOD SECURITY, ENVIRONMENT, AND AGRARIAN REFORM
Failures and Opportunities in Latin America

Jack Hood Vaughn

Jack Hood Vaughn, who is one of the most candid United States public servants to grace corridors of the world's capitals, is also one of the most experienced: onetime director of Peace Corps, former ambassador to both Colombia and Panama, Assistant Secretary of State for Latin America, director of U. S. Agency for International Development missions in four West African countries, past president of both the National Urban Coalition and Planned Parenthood and founding chairman of Conservation International. We weren't sure whether to ask Jack, who is currently serving as environmental counselor for USAID's Regional Office on Central American Policy, to speak on population, politics or conservation as they relate to food security, so he made our lives easy and covered all three, plus a few other topics. Jack's list of lessons learned and opportunities seen in three decades on the front lines of government decision making provide valuable insights for nongovernmental organizations. He discusses the potential pitfalls and opportunities for NGOs in collaborating with bilateral donors, host governments and local groups on food security and conservation interventions. As do Martin and DeWitt, Vaughn concludes that lasting change for the good begins at grassroots.

WE NEED TO COMMUNICATE UNEQUIVOCALLY that food security and environment are in terminal jeopardy as long as the three billion peasants of the world remain unreached by education, and by health and agricultural extension.

When I was a graduate student studying Latin America, the standard textbook was Frank Tannenbaum's *Ten Keys to Latin America*

(New York: Random House, 1966). During the intervening years, those ten keys to understanding Latin America have basically lost their importance or validity. Today, a more rewarding exercise might be to analyze the ten major recent failures affecting quality of life in Latin America to find where new opportunities await, where crucial lessons can be learned, and where old symptoms can be brushed aside and fundamental contradictions exposed.

These ten failures are illustrative of our past follies, fantasies, and myopia. They stem from bad judgement, bad luck, and bad bureaucracy. An awareness of these failures may present us with a better chance to make amends in achieving food security along with environmental balance.

The Lessons of Failure

The Failure of Communism. It would be difficult to overstate the importance for future food security, conservation, and agrarian reform of the new universally admitted failure of communism. Its demise opens the door to new enterprise, new creativity, less government, abolishtion of sterile rhetoric, and faster response to problem resolution. It will enable the new Latin American leadership to revolutionize universities by making them institutions for learning instead of debating. It will bring them back to relevance. For two generations, communism was an unmitigated disaster for Latin American universities and for development. It held the universities hostage to medieval nonsense.

The Failure of Family Planning. The biggest single obstacle and contradiction to rationalizing the use of the world's natural resources and to achieving of food security is the demographic explosion. In 1992, the world will grow by 100,000,000 people. Unfortunately, the United States continues to rain on the world's family planning parade. To cement the U.S. position, ex-U.S. Senator James Buckley was sent to the latest World Population Congress in Mexico City in 1984 with the word that: "We in the United States see no connection between population and development." More than anything else, this U.S. cop-out has been responsible for the recent quasi paralysis in the world's family planning efforts.

The Failure in the Battle against Drugs. Principal among the several factors causing our failure to stop drugs is the one of abandoning the fight to big government. There has been some evidence that big governments can run effective drug *promotion* programs. There is none that governments alone can *stop* effective drug promotion. We can no longer rely on governments to fix the problem. We must look to other approaches and coalitions, other incentives and disincentives—especially at the local level.

The Failure of Agricultural Extension. As director of the Peace Corps, I visited fifty countries a year. In those days, a high percentage of volunteers worked within national agricultural extension services. These services were all patent failures. Then, and ever since, I have been stunned by the world's willingness to passively accept this fact and these classically unproductive systems. If we are forced to make peace with inert and grossly inefficient national agricultural exten sions services in the Third World, then two critical truths become evident:

1. we cannot possibly achieve our food security goals, and
2. there is no hope for bringing higher awareness and technical assistance to the subsistence farmer—possibly the greatest of all threats to the environment in our global efforts to promote sustainable agriculture.

Ten years ago, the flamboyant Commissioner of Agriculture for the state of Texas, Jim Hightower, coauthored a book entitled *Hard Times, Hard Tomatoes.* In it, he pointed out that, in effect, the U.S. Agricultural Extension Service had stopped trying to reach the very small farmer (the one who most needs support) after World War II. Currently, the focus is on the medium-to-large U.S. farmer, providing better farm management methods, better techniques for the use of chemical fertilizers, and promoting the use of larger machinery. Meanwhile, throughout the Third World, one finds a largely bureaucratized, overstaffed, rigid national structure termed "agricultural extension service." A universal misnomer, it extends nothing beyond status quo, job security, and status.

Pick a Third World country in Africa or Latin America and visit a remote agricultural extension office. The odds are overwhelming that you will find an extension agent who is deskbound; his jeep is out of order; and his shelves are full of yellowed pamphlets awaiting distribution to illiterate peasants. No extension takes place. Nobody complains.

Late in the Carter administration, as head of the U.S. foreign aid program for Latin America, I accompanied the administrator of that program, Doug Bennett, to Panama.

Waiting to see the power behind the Panamanian throne, we paid a visit to General Omar Torrijos Herrera at his beach resort on the Pacific coast. As we began our meeting with the general, his first words were: "You gringos are crazy!" After agreeing with him, we asked for some examples. He offered the case of El Salvador, in words something like this:

> *You certainly understand, having been through one of the bloodiest civil wars in modern history from which it took the United States three generations to recover, that the most destabilizing experience a society can go through is a civil war. You should also understand that the second most destabilizing thing that can befall a society is agrarian reform. You gringos must be crazy to insist that El Salvador undertake major agrarian reform during the height of its civil war. And furthermore, you must know that it is impossible for an agrarian reform program to succeed if there is no effective agricultural extension service to support and sustain the newly settled peasant at his time of greatest need, as was the case in El Salvador.*

Nobel laureate and plant breeder Norman Borlaug has noted that only 10 percent of the world's farmers have access to modern technology. If we cannot find ways to bring some technology to the three billion peasant farmers on the world's fringes, there will be no food security, no environmental security, and no political peace.

Maybe the new Mexican model will be a breakthrough. Mexican President Carlos Salinas de Gortari has just announced his intention to abolish the seventy-year-old *ejido* system, which has effectively crippled the country's agricultural sector since the revolution (see Chapter Seven). If Mexico can prevent a new national agricultural extension service from coming in to smother initiative and harden its categories, we may witness a real agricultural miracle during the1990s.

The Failure of Military Aid. In the First, Second, and Third Worlds, all the evidence reflects the ecological disasters wrought by military forces. If there is a peace dividend in the 1990s, it will undoubtedly come in two forms: the stopping of military aid to Third World countries, and major reductions in armed forces and armaments throughout the world. There are two military aid failures over the past forty years that dwarf all others: the failure of U.S. military aid in Vietnam and Soviet military aid in Afghanistan.

The Failure of Economic Aid. The major donors of foreign aid have lent the Third World into bankruptcy. In so doing, they have nearly bankrupted themselves. Their genius for doing this stemmed from relentlessly lending to the public sector, thereby making big government bigger and less efficient.

A second critical deficiency in most economic aid has been a general inability to achieve or motivate replication of successful activities in the field. We haven't been able to get beyond pilot projects.

The Failure of Micromanagement. In my many years working with international nongovernmental organizations (NGOs) and bureaucracies, I have noticed a strong tendency on the part of most NGOs to clamp onto a controlling piece of the action and never let go. After getting the go-ahead and the money, the NGO field office manages it to make sure its project is implemented on time and according to donor home office specifications, and that no money is misspent. Frequently, there is limited effort to involve companion or parallel groups in the country where the project takes place. This is the major cause for pilot projects remaining pilot projects.

There may be more than 2,000 local conservation NGOs in Central America today—up from 300 three years ago. If we cannot involve these local NGOs in food security initiatives, we shall not prevail. If international NGOs, driven by their donors (and USAID is a major one), continue to micromanage projects to a bureaucratic death, we obviously cannot reach out effectively to these new local NGOs.

The Failure of Pilot Projects. About five years ago, a friend of mine analyzed 110 evaluations conducted by outside consultants of USAID designed or supported agricultural extension programs around the world. The evidence was overwhelming that none of these 110 programs had succeeded. The standard response to perceived failure in such initiatives was to launch a new pilot project.

I agree with Peter Drucker: the road to hell is paved with pilot projects. Especially NGO hell. Instead of pilot projects, I believe it is time we began to think in terms of campaigns. A good example of a winning long-term campaign is what UNICEF executive director James Grant has done with the infant-saving oral rehydration program, one that relies heavily on *volunteer* community health workers.

Volunteers basically are the ones who win campaigns—military, political, or other. Volunteers keep us honest and productive.

In his first speech, the current head of the Rockefeller Foundation said, "Identifying issues and starting pilot projects isn't enough anymore. In the 1990s, foundations and NGOs will wield influence only by creating high-impact events that redefine the public debate. Not by funding people and programs on the margins. Not by incrementalism. Not by pilot projects." How does one create a high-impact project? It is probably done by stopping what you are doing. It may help to realize that we do not have that many enemies anymore. We can reach out with new confidence to build new coalitions. Words like merge, join, coalesce, broker, promote, campaign, and volunteer should be the operative verbs for the 1990s. They are great antidotes to micro-management tendencies.

The Failure of Big Government. From Russia to Zaire, from Mexico to Argentina, the worst obstacle to food security, growth, and conservation over the past several decades has been big, bad government. Fortunately, that pendulum has swung back to where nongovernmental initiatives are much more in vogue, and much easier to carry out. Here is the chance NGOs have been waiting for!

The Failure of Conservation. I agree with Robert Rodale, of Rodale organic farms, who believed that conservation is dead and that we really do not understand the nature of the ecological mess we are in. Rodale predicted that all important concepts and initiatives for the future will begin with the letters *RE* (for example, reforestation, recycling, rehabilitation, renovation, renewal, etc.). None of these concepts is a symptom. We must begin thinking *RE*. I urge all readers, in your next blood test, to register *RE* positive.

Former Foreign Minister of Israel, Abba Eban, used to say that men and governments make rational decisions once they have exhausted all the other alternatives. If we are not exhausted by now from having made all those irrational decisions, maybe it is time to start a legitimate campaign for food security.

We no longer have the Communists shouting at the United States in the United Nations. Instead, the Russians are urging the U.S. to privatize faster and to reduce the size of our government (just like the U.S. Republicans!)

The so called "sixty-six nonaligned countries" have gone out of business and now seek alignment in common markets, regional arrangements, and joint ventures.

Environment is in vogue everywhere. It is a rational link between conservation and food security. Since we have exhausted so many futile options in terms of promoting agricultural extension, agrarian reforms, food security, and sustainable agriculture, should we not finally face up to the inherent contradictions and get big government off our back? History shows the best way to do this is to expand our coalitions of volunteers and start a campaign.

Indeed, there is one in the making: as many as 50,000 citizens are expected to participate in the United Nations Conference on Development (UNCED). This would represent probably ten times the number of people involved directly in most past international meetings about the long-term future for the environment.

Traditional forces at the UNCED meeting in Brazil may be tempted to seek easy compromise, consensus, and lowest common denominator identification of major plenary symptoms of ecological disaster: loss of topsoil, deforestation, pollution, global warming, and thinning of layers of ozone. But these symptoms have little to do with the basic causes threatening food security and a livable environment for today and tomorrow.

UNCED and other such conferences must produce a brave and honest analysis of the primal causes: population explosion, illiteracy, poverty, bad government, cattle overgrazing, the military, failure of agricultural extension, and failure of agrarian reform. Resolutions from this conference and its progeny must speak to the highest common denominator. We must finally get beyond symptoms, and deal with basic obstacles and contradictions.

CHAPTER FIVE

THE HUMAN FARM
People-Based Approach to Food Production
and Conservation

Milton Flores and Elías Sánchez

*Moving from ideas and lessons to actions, Honduran Milton Flores,
with a soft voice and tremendous conviction, warns nongovernmental organizations of the folly of trying to deliver improved
agricultural and conservation techniques to poor farmers before
one delivers them an education. As director of the International
Covercrop Clearing House of Tegucigalpa, Honduras, Flores has
pioneered, with success, dissemination of information on "green
manures" (nitrogen-fixing covercrops) and other organic technologies to impoverished hillside farmers of his homeland. Coauthor
Elías Sánchez runs Honduran demonstration farm "Finca Loma
Linda," which trains thousands of farmers annually. Both use
healthy farming techniques as a means, not an end, to help the poor
come to grips with their environment, and thus become better
stewards of it.*

IF THE MIND OF A *campesino* is a desert, his farm will look like a desert.[1]
To overcome perceived conflicts between the objectives of sustainable
development and those of environmental conservation in poor
countries nongovernmental organizations (NGOs) must begin with
proper development of the knowledge, motivation and skill of poor
people responsible for food production. We must give a "human face"
to any food security and conservation program in the world. People
are the problem—not the trees, the soil or even the crops—so it is with
people we must work to care for trees, manage hillsides, and produce
grains.

74

Three Basic Areas of Human Development:
Knowledge, Actions and Consciousness

To better understand the mentality of a *campesino*, let's examine agricultural production in the Honduran hills. Most farmers with whom we work at the International Covercrop Clearing House (CIDICCO), a Honduran NGO, carry out their agricultural production on hilly areas, usually of a more than thirty-degree pitch. These farmers have few land or financial resources, and they lack the knowledge, skills, and mind-set necessary to break their chains of poverty and hopelessness. Mountains cover 81 percent of Honduras, and a great majority of *campesinos* live in these areas and sustain themselves on whatever crops they can eke out of the hills.[2] Numerous NGO and government agricultural and conservation programs have been implemented to protect or develop these fragile slopes.

These programs have used different "institutional strategies" to promote technologies that are supposed to be appropriate for these types of conditions, including food-for-work programs, soil conservation subsidies in cash or in kind, and credit for fertilizers and other agricultural inputs.

If an emphasis on human development has been present in these programs, it has been overshadowed by pursuit of short-term, tangible objectives. The clearest evidence of this shortsightedness is that despite millions of dollars invested into Honduran rural development programs over the past decade, there has been little improvement in literacy, access to schools, child malnutrition or crop marketing for small *campesinos* in the target areas.

When we take a closer look at the people side of the problem, we see project target populations consist of:
- the economically poorest persons
- the least educated or trained persons
- those with the greatest history of failures
- those who are most disillusioned by politicians, technicians, and even development agencies
- those most attached to traditions
- those with the greatest number of children
- those more vulnerable to diseases.

By understanding these demographics we can see that the environmental degradation of the *campesinos'* farms is only another expression of the personal and spiritual degradation of those who work the land. Poor farmers, applying meager knowledge, take action based on their own desperate reality. As stated: if the mind of a *campesino* is a desert, his farm will look like a desert!

A "human" farm requires that a farmer increase awareness of his or her relationship to the land in order to become a proponent of positive, sustainable development. The following three aspects of human development are essential for successful programs in agriculture, health, reforestation, soil conservation, or any other grassroots program aimed at bringing permanent societal change.

Useful Knowledge. The most useful knowledge allows a person to understand cause and effect. For example, in agriculture, we must help farmers understand, in a clear manner, relationships between mountains, trees, rain, loss of soil, low yields, poverty, health, education, and oppression. The measurement of this goal contrasts with those of many NGOs', which are expressed in terms of kilometers of contour ditches, numbers of trees planted, and numbers of rural silos built. Useful knowledge is that which helps farmers to make better use of local resources, wisdom, traditions, and values. It will help farmers solve a specific problem and apply that experience to new situations.

Useful Awareness. The awakening of a person's consciousness will make him or her dissatisfied with his or her present economic and social condition. This awakening will motivate the farmer to try to change his or her condition, and share her or his new vision with others.

In CIDICCO programs in Honduras, a key sign of a good agricultural leader is his or her willingness to volunteer to teach others what she or he is learning from the program. Such initiative may eventually bring the volunteer opportunities to earn a modest salary as part of a paid extension team.

Knowledge and Awareness Translated into Concrete Actions. A good program enables farmers to get involved in simple experiments that may help them modify their techniques and gain new knowledge.

Practical Implications of This Perspective

To maintain productivity and ensure the well being of people while making a rational use of natural resources, one must do more than simply set global, national, or personal objectives or policy. One must state these objectives and policies in human terms. Politicians must take action to help train and educate poor farmers if they wish to promote environmental conservation. They must consider people development a politically viable objective. In addition, policy makers must find a means to create trust and establish healthy communication between extension workers, academia, and suspicious *campesinos*, who for generations have been exploited and ignored.

The means will involve working through NGOs and government agencies. *How* then can NGOs and government agencies build bridges? Try the following suggestions.

Practice What You Preach. In Honduras, no agronomist can be a good extensionist if he cannot harvest good corn himself. Our experience has demonstrated that one of the best ways to get people interested in a particular program, without external incentives, is to let them observe the extensionist's agricultural work.

Programs use different strategies. Sometimes extensionists rent, buy or make other arrangements to obtain a piece of land similar in soil, topography, and water limitations to that of the majority of the *campesinos* in the target area. The idea is to actually practice the technique as part of a learning-by-doing process, and eventually show visitors what is being done. An extensionist *has* to have his or her own plot to gain the respect of the people with whom he or she is working.

Start Small. One needs to begin with none too ambitious objectives and goals. The main objective, initially, is to gain the respect of the people and get them interested and willing to receive new ideas. More importantly, one needs to begin conceptually, technologically, and financially "small."

1. *Conceptually.* Most peasant farmers cannot assimilate many new concepts simultaneously. Concepts should be introduced one at a time with concrete examples. For example, if talking about organic matter and humus, prepare a piece of land where *campesinos* can see, feel, and touch organic matter and humus. If talking about how crops respond to organic fertilizers, use the fertilizers on a small plot of corn.

2. *Technologically.* We have mentioned that "useful knowledge" teaches farmers to use local resources. Many times a positive impact can be obtained with only minor modifications to traditional practices. Successes achieved in this manner will reinforce a peasant's sense of self-worth, encourage his or her more active participation in an experiment, and augment his or her feeling of ownership in the technique.[3]

3. *Financially.* Changes that are perceived to be expensive or too costly in terms of time or labor will not easily be accepted. Another advantage of starting financially small is avoiding overspending on sophisticated equipment or program overhead. However, a good program must have enough resources to

deploy staff, pay salaries according to the country's standards, and maintain basic facilities.

Respect the Culture of the People. No matter how peculiar the native practices, technologies, or traditions may seem, there are important reasons behind them. We often hear comments about damage caused to the environment by the traditional Third World practice of burning fields before planting. But, a closer look at this practice shows some positive effects: fire does control insects, destroy undesirable weeds and release certain amounts of nutrients into the soil.

Discussing the positive results of such a practice can lead to a discussion of alternative practices for achieving the same results without negative side effects; for example, discussing how certain plant residues also increase the fertility of soils and improve the soil's physical condition. As people better understand the "ends" of their actions, they will more readily modify the "means."

Work as a Servant. People should *see* that an extensionist or development worker is truly interested in serving them. A good extensionist should be willing to work in less than desirable conditions. His or her enthusiasm will stimulate interest and make people willing to listen.

Build Local Leadership. Building local leadership to take over rural extension activities communicates to *campesinos* that they are capable of becoming a substitute for a foreign actor. No matter how well or poorly educated the NGO foreign actor is, *campesinos* will consider measuring up to him or her an accomplishment. Local leaders should be trained to step in as extensionists after program staff leave a foreign region.

A promising leader will share what he is learning with his neighbors without expecting to receive a salary. A good leader will put into practice himself what he has learned and will be eager to learn more.

A Typical Example: The Use of Legumes on a "Human" Farm

In recent years, CIDICCO has done hundreds of consultations regarding the use of legumes in traditional agricultural systems. More and more people are realizing the important role these plants have played in balancing agricultural ecosystems and are seeing their potential for improving small farmers' agricultural systems. Two brief examples follow.

The Use Of Choreque. Choreque is the popular name given to the legume (*Lathyrus nigrivalvis*) in the western state of Chimaltenango,

Guatemala. This plant grows extremely well at altitudes of 5700 to 7600 feet above sea level. *Choreque* has been widely intercropped with corn by *campesinos*. Farmers have observed that this association improves the fertility of the soil, which results in better corn yields.

According to data obtained from a Guatemalan researcher[4] *choreque* can produce an extraordinary yield of 100 tons per hectare in a six-month period. It contains 2.93 percent nitrogen, which it releases into the soil, providing a critical element in the agricultural system. This plant's residues, under this region's conditions, could substitute for the use of chemical nitrogen.

The Use of Velvetbean (Mucuna pruriens). Velvetbean is another legume widely used by small farmers in Central America. In some regions, it is traditionally intercropped with corn or planted throughout a corn field in the course of crop rotation.

This legume can be cultivated in a wide variety of environments, and at up to 1500 meters above sea level. It adapts well to humid tropical conditions and to more moderate climates. It can be used under cropping conditions of small poor farmers or on larger commercial farms.

This plant is greatly strengthening the sustainability of small farmers' agricultural systems by:

- contributing up to 200 kilograms of nitrogen per hectare per year[5];
- producing tremendous amounts of biomass (between thirty-five and thirty-seven tons/hectare in a period of four months;[6]
- reducing labor costs of weeding and land preparation;
- as much as tripling yields per area after continuous use;
- providing additional protein to complement poor families' diet;
- providing fodder and protein for animal feedings;

Given these important technical considerations, one could be easily misled to focus too much energy and too many resources on extension work and/or research that focuses on use of legumes as a separate soil conservation activity. By doing that, one would neglect other more important objectives of the "human" farm.

Instead, these legume experiments should be used as a tool to open a deeper process of development education. By discussing with peasant farmers the lessons learned in their actual field trials of legumes, extensionists should find great opportunity for more comprehensive dialogues, ones that will, sooner or later, include other topics directly related to the quality of life of the *campesinos'* family.

If one fails to focus on human development objectives, one may create new waves in agricultural development, but no real tides of change. If the practice of using legumes were to become only an agricultural project input, it would eventually join the ranks of other faded technologies. To bring about *campesinos'* true acceptance and use of these practices, the technique must relate to a permanent *lifestyle* change.

Other Considerations

Many agencies say they are people-centered. Unfortunately, the majority of these agencies are really concerned with achieving physical goals: numbers of trees planted, numbers of latrines built, or numbers of loans granted by the end of a period.

The fundamental objective of any real development program should be to contribute to human development. This can involve improving agricultural practices, conserving natural resources, or improving community health at the farm, regional, or national level, but it must not stop there. Indeed, the real challenge facing NGOs is to design programs that deeply consider local human needs and can bring about permanent life-style and attitudinal changes. Without such human transformation, environmental protection activity will stop when an agency leaves. No more trees will be planted, contour ditches will grow thick with grasses and soil, and the latrines will be used for grain storage. Any physical achievements toward strengthening food security through land conservation will become part of the target Community's "development museum."[7]

A Final Word

- NGOs must elicit clear objectives from private and governmental agencies, ones that show a primary interest in human development.
- More NGOs should publicly advocate people-centered development as the best method of truly increasing food security and environmental conservation.
- We must see, in the literature and language of communities, nations and international NGOs, acknowledgement that people are the starting place for sustaining the land—not

trees, not soil and not crops. We must work with the "human" farm, with those who will take care of the trees, manage the hillsides, and produce the grains, not just now, but for generations.

Notes

1. The idea has been taken from Elías Sánchez and Milton Flores in "La Finca Humana: Principios Practicas Agricultura Sostenible Laderas," CIDICCO, 1991. "*Campesino*" is the Spanish word for peasant.
2. Various. *Perfil Ambiental De Honduras* (Honduras: SECPLAN, 1989), 45.
3. Roland Bunch, *Two Ears of Corn* (Oklahoma: World Neighbors, 1982), 98.
4. Villatoro Rudy Antonio. *Evaluacion del Efecto del Choreque (Lathyrus nigrivalvis) Como Abono Verde a Cinco Niveles de Fertilizacion Quimica En Maiz* (Guatemala: Universidad De San Carlos, 1977).
5. Data obtained by researchers of the TROPSOIL program of Cornell University, 1990.
6. CIDICCO observations in Finca Monte Libano, Choluteca, Honduras, 1991.
7. Observation of Juan Sanchez, president of CIED (Research, Education and Development Center), Lima, Peru.

CHAPTER SIX

THE LONG AND SHORT OF IT
Relationships Between Coping Strategies, Food Security
and Environmental Degradation in Africa

Timothy R. Frankenberger and Daniel M. Goldstein

*Tim Frankenberger, farming systems research specialist, and Dan
Goldstein, research assistant at the Office of Arid Lands Studies,
University of Arizona, have practical advice for helping nongovernmental organizations (NGOs) link poor people's short-term household food needs to long-term needs for environmental conservation.
An expert in rapid rural appraisal, household food security, and
information systems for famine mitigation, Tim is a consultant to
various United Nations and North American development agencies.
Dan is a doctoral candidate in anthropology with interests in household production systems and state-community relationships. Their
matrices and graphs in this chapter are useful tools for helping NGOs
think through appropriate interventions in famine-prone regions.*

HOUSEHOLDS DO NOT RESPOND ARBITRARILY to variability in food supply.
People who live in conditions that put their main source of income at
recurrent risk will develop self-insurance strategies to minimize risk to
their food security and livelihood.[1] This careful forward planning,
which can be termed a coping strategy, is fundamental to the survival
of small farmers throughout Africa. Development practitioners concerned with helping small farm households improve their food security must begin by understanding the strategies employed by these
households in coping with the risk of hunger.

In adapting to an unpredictable, fluctuating environment, farmers
may adopt coping strategies that are destructive to that environment.
The dilemma facing small farm households when coping with threats
to household food security involves a basic trade-off between short-

term subsistence and long-term sustainability. In a context of food insecurity, when the viability of the household as a productive and reproductive unit is threatened by food shortage, farmers often must employ strategies that increase immediate income sources and subsistence levels, but that have detrimental consequences for the natural environment.

This paper presents an analysis of farmer coping strategies and how they are employed in maintaining household food security. After a discussion of short-term coping strategies used by small farmers, we look at the long-term impacts such practices can have on local environments, and suggest how these strategies may serve as indicators of an impending food crisis. Given that there is a patterned response on the part of households to any food crisis, timely interventions could provide limited resource families alternative means to meet their food security needs before turning to unsustainable strategies. This paper outlines the issues and procedures for establishing a decentralized food security monitoring system. Such a system promotes timely interventions that contribute to sustainable management of natural resources.

Household Food Security and the Environment:
An Historical Perspective

Although there is a strong relationship between poor people's household food security and environmental conservation, until recently there has been limited attention given to the nature of this relationship.[2] Food security is defined by the World Bank as "access by all people at all times to enough food for an active and healthy life."[3] Putting the concept into practice at the national level is not the same as at the household level. At the national level, food security entails adequate food supplies through local production and food imports. However, adequate availability of food at the national level does not necessarily translate into even distribution across the country, nor equal access among all households. Household food security means the availability of adequate food (as in culturally acceptable, safe and nutritionally adequate) as well as the ability of the household to have stable access to such food through its own production or purchase (see Figure 6.1). Thus, availability and stable access are keys to household food security. Households will have stable access to food if they have viable means for procuring food (either produced or purchased) that does not lead to environmental

FIGURE 6.1 Conceptual Framework for Household Food Security

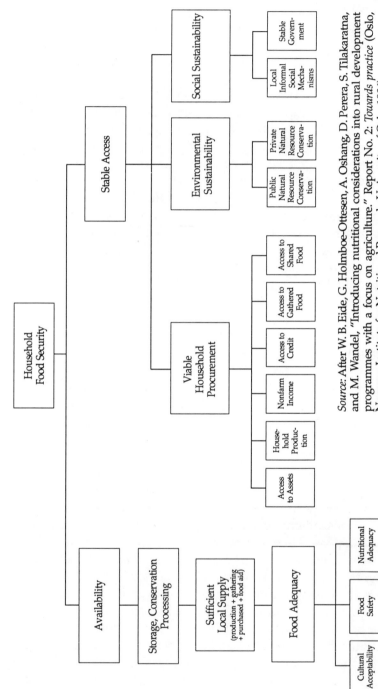

Source: After W. B. Eide, G. Holmboe-Ottesen, A. Oshang, D. Perera, S. Tilakaratna, and M. Wandel, "Introducing nutritional considerations into rural development programmes with a focus on agriculture." Report No. 2: *Towards practice* (Oslo, Norway: Institute for Nutritional Research, University of Oslo, 1986).

degradation. Stable access is also influenced by local, informal social mechanisms (for example, food sharing networks), that buffer households from periodic shocks, and by the stability of the national government.

In spite of this strong link, policy formulation for household food security and environmental sustainability has continued along parallel tracks since the 1970s.[4] Linking these two factors has been difficult, partially because much of the relevant work has been carried out across several disciplines and areas of research, where interactions between food security and environmental issues are rarely addressed directly. The convergence of food security and environmental interests has come about mainly through a focus on vulnerable groups experiencing food shortages during the drought that plagued much of Africa in the early 1980s. Many development practitioners began to realize that strengthening food security required increasing environmental conservation, and conservation could not be achieved if the people who were dependent on natural resources for their livelihoods were ignored.[5] By focusing on the way households cope with food shortages, it became apparent that in times of vulnerability these households relied heavily on natural resources outside their usual production system or intensified the exploitation of resources already in use.[6] Thus, the links between household food security and environmental use were addressed explicitly through studies that focused on coping strategies.

Coping Strategies and the Small Farm Household

In attempting to maintain food security and productive potential, households employ a variety of coping strategies to deal with uncertain or worsening environmental conditions. Within a given strategy, households will pursue an array of responses for ensuring against food scarcity and famine. Examples of such responses include dispersed grazing, changes in cropping and planting practices, migration to towns in search of urban employment, increased petty commodity production, collection of wild foods, use of interhousehold transfers and loans, use of credit from merchants and money lenders, migration to other rural areas for employment, rationing of current food consumption, sale of possessions (such as jewelry), sale of firewood and charcoal, consumption of food distributed through relief programs, sale of productive assets, breakup of the household, and distress migration.[7] Evidence from Africa and Asia has demonstrated that common patterns in coping strategies can be identified.[8]

In analyzing varieties of coping strategies, it is important to distinguish between two types of assets that farmers have at their disposal. Assets that represent stores of value for liquidation are acquired during noncrisis years as a form of savings and self-insurance; these may include small livestock or personal possessions such as jewelry. A second set of assets are those that play a key role in generating income. These are less liquid as stores of value, and are much more costly to the farm household in their disposal. Households first will dispose of assets held as stores of value before disposing of productive assets.[9]

Most initial responses to actual or potential food shortages are extensions of practices conducted in some measure during normal years to adapt to rainfall variability.[10] Traditional methods of handling risk can be divided into routine risk minimizing practices and loss management mechanisms.[11] Risk minimizing practices are adjustments to production and resource use before and during a production season. This involves such practices as diversification of resources and enterprises, and adjustments within cropping systems. Crop-centered diversification can include choosing crops with varying maturation periods, different sensitivities to environmental fluctuations, and flexible end use of products.[12] Farmers will also reduce production risks by exploiting vertical, horizontal, and temporal dimensions of the natural resource base. Vertical adjustments involve planting at different elevations in a topographic sequence. Spatial risk adjustment includes planting in different microenvironments or intercropping. Temporal risk adjustments involve staggering planting times.[13] Adjustments may also include extension of farming to marginal areas or overuse of a particular plot, practices that can have a destructive effect on the natural environment.

Loss management mechanisms include farmers' responses to lower than expected crop production caused by natural hazards.[14] Reductions in crop production can be compensated through nonfarm income, the sale of produce durables (livestock), the management of stocks and reserves, seasonal migration, and reciprocal obligations among households. Overexploitation of certain natural resources (forest reserves, for example) for market sale may also be part of a loss management strategy.

In communities marked by landholding and income inequalities, household responses are not the same.[15] Indeed, identical climatic conditions can affect households of varied economic levels to different degrees. Conditions that produce seasonal shortages for some families mean famine for others. Poorer households, having smaller holdings and a weaker resource base, are more vulnerable to stress than are wealthier households, and begin to suffer earlier when food shortages hit. The poor resort to early sale of livestock, pledge farms, incur debt, sell labor, and borrow grain at higher interest rates.[16] In essence, crop failures reveal, rather than cause, the fragile nature of food security among vulnerable rural families. At the same time, prosperous households buy stock at deflated prices in conditions of oversupply, sell or lend grain to needy farmers, purchase wage labor at depressed rates, and purchase land.[17] Thus, during a food crisis, a cycle of accumulation and decapitalization can occur simultaneously within a single community.

Patterns of coping strategies can be diagramed to show the sequence of responses farm households typically employ when faced with a food crisis (Figure 6.2). In the earliest stages of a crisis, farmers employ the types of risk minimizing and loss management strategies discussed above. These typically involve a low commitment of domestic resources, enabling speedy recovery once the crisis has eased. As the crisis persists, farmers are increasingly forced into a greater commitment of resources just to meet subsistence needs, a strategy that becomes less reversible the longer the crisis persists. The final failure to cope with a food crisis is marked by permanent out-migration from the region.[18]

Recent studies have found that the range of coping strategies pursued by farm families in drought prone areas may be changing over time.[19] Three major trends appear to be developing. First, risk minimizing agricultural strategies appear to be narrowing in some locations (for example, in Kenya), as repeated sales and reacquisition have depleted domestic and productive asset levels. In these areas, agricultural coping strategies are being replaced by strategies that diversify income sources through off-farm employment and nonagricultural production.[20] These nonfarm strategies often include practices that are known to be environmentally damaging, but which provide a last resort in crisis conditions. Second, strategies that relied on social support and reciprocity for overcoming food deficits are eroding due to the integration of individual households into the cash economy.[21] Third, a shift has been observed in the responsibility for coping with drought from the individual household and local community toward the national government through famine relief programs.[22] This trend is due in large part to the reduction in response flexibility of small farm households.[23]

FIGURE 6.2
Household Responses to Food Shortages

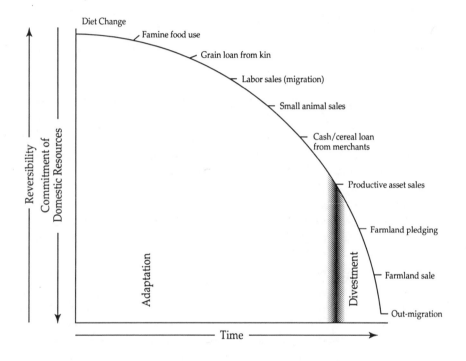

Source: Adapted from Michael Watts, *Silent Violence: Food, Famine and Peasantry in Northern Nigeria.* Copyright 1983 The Regents of the University of California.

Coping Strategies and Environmental Degradation

While coping strategies may be seen in the short term as functional adaptations to uncertain conditions and hence beneficial, some commonly practiced strategies may have dire consequences for the natural environment in the long run. Particularly for poorer farmers with limited resource endowments, the process of maintaining household viability may be exacted at the expense of their natural surroundings. Poor people often occupy ecologically vulnerable areas such as marginal dry lands, tropical forests, and hilly areas.[24] As drought conditions worsen and conditions of food insecurity persist, the range of options available to resource poor farmers becomes more limited and inflexible. In such situations, questions of long-term environmental sustainability become secondary. Day-to-day survival demands the use of any food procurement strategy available. In areas like the Sahel, where persistent drought is coupled with increasing population levels, less destructive practices are more quickly exhausted, hastening the onset of desperation strategies.

The exploitation of common property resources (CPRs) is particularly important for resource poor farmers for meeting household food security needs. Wild leaves, roots, grains, bush meat and forest products provide additional food sources, buffer seasonal shortages, and provide alternative sources of income.[25] These resources are relied upon heavily during times of stress.[26] Therefore, the degradation of CPRs and loss through the encroachment of privatized agriculture has disproportionately affected the food security of the poor.

Women are often more vulnerable to the effects of environmental degradation than men because they are often more involved in the collection of common property resources.[27] Since women make a greater contribution to household food security than men, a decline in women's access to resources may have a significant impact on the nutritional status of the household.

Coping strategies that may promote environmental degradation include cutting trees to make charcoal, overharvesting wild foods, overgrazing grasslands, and increased planting in marginal areas. All of these strategies may degrade soil conditions and augment problems of soil erosion.[28] Farmers often realize the damage their actions cause to the environment upon which their livelihood depends. However, as drought conditions worsen and food insecurity persists, the range of options narrows, leaving very few strategies for putting food in their children's bellies.

The unsustainable strategies that resource poor farmers employ can serve as indicators of an impending crisis. As farmers exhaust the strategies that are available in the early stages of food crisis (for example, reduction of consumption levels, harvesting of wild foods, changes in cropping patterns, sale of small livestock and household valuables), they begin to dispose of productive assets in an attempt to stave off total dissolution of the household unit (see Figure 6.2). Should these strategies prove ineffective, farmers may then resort to the more destructive practices.[29]

Awareness of local coping strategies and ongoing monitoring of local conditions and of trends in strategies being employed (for example, exhaustion of assets, depletion of stores, increased migration) can alert development agents to areas where immediate interventions may be needed. These areas can be targeted for development plans that enable farm families to prolong the effectiveness of nondegrading coping strategies.[30]

Establishing a Decentralized Food Security Monitoring System

The generalized patterns of coping strategies discussed above find practical application as tools for food security monitoring. Rather than focusing strictly on the outcome of farmer responses to production constraints and food crises, development practitioners can develop methods to monitor the processes by which households cope with food insecurity. Monitoring these processes will improve famine early warning systems as well as guide interventions for increasing farm productivity.

Building upon the work of the World Food Program (WFP), there are three types of indicators that can be monitored to detect changing coping responses that suggest worsening conditions and heightened food insecurity.

Leading indicators (WFP refers to these as *early indicators*) are changes in conditions and responses prior to the onset of decreased food access. Examples of such indicators include:

1. crop failures (due to inadequate rainfall, poor access to seed and other inputs, pest damage, etc.);
2. sudden deterioration of rangeland conditions or condition of livestock (for example, unusual migration movements, unusual number of animal deaths, large number of young female animals being offered for sale);
3. significant deterioration in local economic conditions (for example, increases in price of grain, unseasonable disappearance

of essential food stuffs, increases in unemployment among laborers and artisans, unusually low levels of household foodstocks); and

4. significant accumulation of livestock by some households (due to depressed prices caused by oversupply).

Leading indicators can provide signs of an impending problem and may call for a detailed situation analysis to determine the extent of the problem, causes, and need for monitoring.

Concurrent indicators (WFP calls these *stress indicators*) occur simultaneously with decreased access to food. Examples of such indicators are:

1. larger than normal migrations of able-bodied family members in search of food or work;
2. appearances in the market of unusual amounts of personal and capital goods, such as jewelry, farm implements, livestock (draft animals);
3. unusual increases in land sales or mortgages;
4. increases in the number of people seeking credit;
5. increased dependence on wild foods;
6. reduction in the number of meals; and
7. increased reliance on interhousehold exchanges.

Concurrent indicators can be assessed while carrying out situational analyses using rapid rural appraisals. Once the nature and extent of the problems have been confirmed, interventions can be introduced that focus on the causes or mitigate the effects.

Trailing indicators (WFP calls these *late outcome indicators*) occur after food access has declined. They reflect the extent to which the well-being of particular households and communities has been affected. In addition to signs of malnutrition and high rates of morbidity and mortality, trailing indicators include increased land degradation, land sales, consumption of seed stocks and permanent out-migration. All of these indicators are signs that the household has failed to cope with the food crisis.

Focusing on coping strategies reveals the actual behaviors of farm households that adverse climatic or market conditions have provoked. Such an orientation allows for ongoing monitoring of the processes by which people adjust to changing circumstances.

Community Participation

Focusing on household coping strategies as an essential part of a decentralized food security monitoring system will enable communities to actively participate in monitoring efforts. By compiling this information on household responses, a system can be established based on indigenous strategies for coping with household food insecurity. Local community members can be trained to use an easily learned system for monitoring indicators. Although this system will rely heavily on intuitive assessments by local monitors, information will be collected on standard indicator categories for targeted interventions by the national government. These can be replicated should there be changes in project personnel. Some examples of these indicators are changes in market prices for staples, changes in the type of assets being sold (liquid vs. productive), increased out-migration, increased environmental degradation, and greater reliance on wild foods. Indicator categories would be grouped according to the three types of indicators discussed above (that is, leading, concurrent, trailing).

Complementarity to Early Warning Systems

To effectively monitor the food situation for a given region, systems must be established that can effectively identify those areas that may be experiencing an emergency (early warning), and that can gauge the magnitude of the potential emergency (assessment). Early warning systems such as the Famine Early Warning System (FEWS) and the Global Information and Early Warning System (GIEWS) operated by the Food and Agriculture Organization (FAO) have been very effective in accomplishing the first task, through use of satellite remote sensing, but have not been as successful accomplishing the second. The proposed food security monitoring system complements these national early warning systems by providing more fine tuning of assessments on a localized level.

Recognizing that households pass through different stages in coping strategies will help planners identify key indicators for early warning of impending food crises. A thorough understanding of these coping strategies will enable development agencies to more accurately interpret consumption indicators such as asset sales, price movements, and levels of undernutrition.[31] Famine warning systems need to be localized because few indices are universal indicators of impending famine.

NGO Involvement

To effectively establish food security monitoring systems in food deficit areas and to implement appropriate interventions, nongovernmental organization (NGO) involvement is essential. A number of NGOs have been very active in creating localized monitoring systems over the past several years.[32] This work often began as part of emergency relief assistance and then evolved into development assistance with a capability for early response to food shortages.

Experiences in Ethiopia have made it apparent that maintaining an NGO presence in disaster prone areas is critical for adequate response to food shortages. CARE, Catholic Relief Services (CRS), World Vision (WV), Save the Children, and Food for the Hungry all have large commitments in disaster prone countries. Such a presence provides a basis for mobilization and expansion of food assistance. Almost all of these groups maintain food stocks, trucks, warehouses, experienced staff, and good relationships with local communities. This logistical support is vital to timely interventions.

NGOs also have considerable experience in promoting natural resource management improvements. This experience provides valuable input into programs aimed at soil conservation, water harvesting, and reestablishment of forest reserves. WV has been actively involved in promoting such efforts in Mali.[33] NGOs have also made an impact in training local populations in extension practices. CARE and Food for the Hungry personnel are involved with training people from local communities in Ethiopia in extension activities related to soil conservation. NGOs also could provide training for local community members in monitoring consumption indicators.

Linking Short-Term Food Security and Long-Term Environmental Concerns in the Design of Interventions

One critical area where household food security and environmental objectives may conflict is in the time required to obtain a return on investment. Food security enhancing activities usually require payoffs over a much shorter time frame than resource base enhancing practices.[34] It is at the household level that this conflict between the pursuit of short-term food security and longer-term environmental sustainability are most apparent. Policy interventions that address the dual objectives of household food security and environmental

preservation need to carefully consider this distinction.[35] Assessments of proposed policy interventions should:
1. measure the food security costs of environmental initiatives and the environmental costs of food security enhancing practices;
2. identify ways to compensate for the food security costs of environmental conservation; and
3. explore options for reinforcing indigenous coping strategies that insure food security in ways that do not degrade the environment.[36] An example of a program that has addressed these dual objectives is a WV-run food-for-work/cash-for-work program for pastoralists in Mali (see Case One, Appendix I).

Development practitioners should also use agro-ecosystems analysis in the design of interventions. Conway[37] defines an agro-ecosystem as:

an ecological and socioeconomic system comprising domesticated plants and/or animals and the people who husband them, intended for the purpose of producing food, fiber, or other agricultural products.

From a development perspective, an effective agro-ecosystem is one which aims to increase "social value," the capacity of a system to produce needed goods and services and its ability to satisfy human needs in an equitable manner. The social value of an agro-ecosystem is characterized by four factors[38]:
1. productivity (a measure of valued production);
2. stability (the amount of variation in the system when faced with small disruptions in production);
3. sustainability (the ability to maintain productivity when faced with major disruptions); and
4. equitability (the evenness of distribution among the human population).

Any proposed intervention must consider the impact of that intervention on these four factors. Again, this will involve attention to the trade-off between short-term household and long-term environmental demands. The immediate needs of local communities or individual farm families may prompt interventions aimed at increasing the productivity of the agro-ecosystem.

However, this increase cannot be accomplished at the expense of stable and sustainable production or equitable distribution of output. Similarly, interventions that target longer-term environmental considerations and systemic sustainability must consider the food security needs of local people. Incorporating these considerations in project design will improve the likelihood of local adoption of interventions, and thus improve the chances of environmental benefits being secured down the road.

Interventions

Interventions to improve household food security in the long term in Africa should target natural resource management strategies that enable farmers to maintain or return to sustainable agricultural practices. The fact that some farmers are turning to nonsustainable strategies indicates that traditional controls on resource management have broken down,[39] and can signal areas where interventions may be appropriate. Table 6.1 details land resource initiatives that have been pursued in the Sudano-Sahelian zone of West and Central Africa. In addition, several other alternative interventions have been identified by Davies et al.[40] that address the household food security aspects of natural resource management initiatives (see Table 6.2). More specifically, the following interventions merit close attention.

Food-for-Work/Cash-for-Work to Promote
Natural Resource Improvement and Management

Food-for-work/cash-for-work (FFW/CFW) programs can be implemented in food emergency situations in such a way as to address food security, employment, and environmental concerns simultaneously.[41] During drought years, relief efforts can be instituted that target resource improvement and promote better resource management. Rather than an outright distribution of relief aid, FFW/CFW programs use donated food as payment (either in kind or, through monetization, in cash) for productive labor by relief recipients. While providing employment for the rural poor, such programs also can be implemented to promote efforts in soil conservation, water harvesting, reestablishment of forest reserves, and other development projects aimed at restoring degraded resources and improving agricultural productive potential. These programs not only provide relief during crises, but they do so in ways that expand the potential of indigenous coping strategies to deal with the crisis and forestall liquidation of productive assets.

TABLE 6.1   Land Resource Initiatives in the Sudano-Sahelian Zone

Initiative	Land Resource Targets						
	Soil Conservation	Soil Fertility	Water Conservation	Forestry/ Agro-forestry	Agriculture	Pasture & Vegetation	Biodiversity
Water retention dams	●		●	●	●	●	
Irrigation dams		●	●		●		
Antisalt barriers		●	●		●		●
Microcatchments	●		●	●	●		
Channel protection dams	●		●		●		
Small channel dams	●		●		●		
Vegetation strips	●	●	●			●	●
Contour plowing & tied ridges	●	●	●		●	●	
Diversion bands	●				●		
Windbreaks	●			●	●		
Tree lines	●			●		●	●
Live fences	●			●	●	●	●
Border plantings				●	●		
Dune stabilization	●					●	●

TABLE 6.1   Land Resource Initiatives in the Sudano-Sahelian Zone (continued)

Initiative	Soil Conservation	Soil Fertility	Water Conservation	Forestry/ Agro-forestry	Agriculture	Pasture & Vegetation	Biodiversity
Compost pits		●		●	●		
Compost stables		●		●	●		
Wells & gardens		●	●		●		●
Natural forest management	●			●			
Infield planting	●			●		●	●
Cooperative woodlots				●			
Private woodlots				●			
Nurseries				●		●	●
Fire management	●	●		●	●	●	●
National parks						●	●
Sacred woodlots				●		●	●
Crop introduction		●	●		●		●
Improved stoves				●		●	

Source: R. M. Caldwell, "Land Resource Management in Sudano-Sahelian Belt of West and Central Africa: A Practical View." A draft report prepared for the United Nations Sudano-Sahelian Office, New York, N.Y., 1991.

TABLE 6.2 Possible Environmental Scenarios Caused by the Pursuit of Food Security: Effects and Policy Options

Environmental problem	Content	Cause (how pursuing food affects environment)	Effect (how environmental problems in turn affect food security)	Policy options that negatively affect food security	Alternative policy options
Desertification	• population pressure • increasing land area under cash crop production • debt crisis • government policies encouraging cash crop production, subsidizing inputs, etc. • growing differentiation • declining rainfall in some areas	• cultivation of increasingly marginal land • overintensive crop production (reduction in fallow periods, etc.) • production of deleterious cash crops	• greater risk, declining resistance to drought • some food security when land does produce	• fines for malpractice • restricted access • forced resettlement without compensation	• land redistribution • diversification of economy • change economic incentives • land tenure policies
Soil	• male out-migration • declining household labor (therefore unable to carry out soil conserving farming techniques) • changing rainfall patterns	• cultivation of increasingly marginal land • male migration to work in cash cropping or industry • deforestation	• declining agricultural productivity levels • downstream effect on fisheries/marine life/wildlife • loss of land (for example, hills) • greater risk and variability	• land forcibly taken out of cultivation	• encourage tree planting, water harvesting, or other soil conservation techniques through government incentives or credit to farmers • incentives to reduce male out-migration
Degradation of Pastures	• population pressure • traditional pasture management systems breaking down • falling terms of trade • competition with agricultural production/urban growth/game parks, etc. • drought reduces pasture availability	• number of people relying on pasture increases • overexpansion of herd sizes • modified transhumance patterns	• overgrazing keeps herds alive in drought years so capital stock remains • reduces viability of herd in long-term • reduces long-term carrying capacity of pasture	• fines • restricted access • sedentarization • head tax on livestock • government stipulation of transhumance routes	• incentives to de-stock • land tenure • price support for livestock

TABLE 6.2 Possible Environmental Scenarios Caused by the Pursuit of Food Security: Effects and Policy Options (continued)

Environmental problem	Content (how pursuing food affects environment)	Cause (how pursuing food affects environment)	Effect (how environmental problems in turn affect food security)	Policy options that negatively affect food security	Alternative policy options
Humid tropical deforestation	• international debt burden • population pressure and unequal access to land • pricing policies favoring export/cash crop production at expense of subsistence crops	• resettlement schemes of landless (helping food security in short term) • cattle ranching prospects and large-scale cash cropping	• increases short-term food security for some sectors • induces food insecurity for indigenous forest populations and forest product users	• fines/restrictions for local forest product users	• greater restrictions for MNCs • redistribution of land • grant land rights to indigenous people • buffer zones, forest block management for different users • community managed extractive reserves
Loss of nonforest trees	• government interferences • CPR management systems • population pressure • increasing differentiation and declining access to natural resources among certain sectors • urban fuel wood demands	• cultivation of increasingly marginal land • male migration to work in cash cropping or industry • deforestation	• people seeking to satisfy immediate nutritional ind income needs jeopardizes long-term food security • long-term soil degradation, declining fertility	• fines • restricted areas • forces tree planting when labor is scarce	• planting of useful trees (for example, agro-forestry) • alternative energy sources • new technologies, stoves, etc.
Loss of wildlife	• increase in pressure on limited resources • environmental degradation • food insecurity • inequitable land distribution • breakdown of CPR mechanisms	• number of people relying on pasture increases • overexpansion of herd sizes • modified transhumance patterns	• overgrazing keeps herds alive in drought years so capital stock remains • reduces viability of herd in long-term • reduces long-term carrying capacity of pasture	• fines • restricted access • hunting for wealthy urban elite • tourism driven protection	• reduction of food insecurity • policies aimed at reducing poverty and providing alternative income sources • reinvestment of tourist revenue into local community • community managed extractive reserves

Source: S. Davies, M. Leach and R. David, "Food Security and the Environment: Conflict or Complementarity," *IDS Discussion Paper* (Brighton, England: Institute for Development Studies, U. of Sussex, 1991).

FFW/CFW programs incorporate the dilemma of short- and long-term trade-offs. In determining program objectives, planners must consider the inherent trade-off between the dual benefits of public works programs: short-term employment provision versus long-term resource restoration. Though public works programs can have important roles in crisis mitigation, it is important to recognize that the effectiveness of these programs lies in their ability to restore resources and improve infrastructure while providing aid to the needy. Public works are perhaps best regarded as providing a transition from immediate food insecurity to more sustainable development over time.

Strengthening Local Community Support Networks for Buffering against Periodic Shocks

One system that enables greater flexibility for small households facing food shortages is the local system of mutual obligations and interhousehold transfers that typically exists in an agrarian community. In the initial stages of food shortage, a household can call upon other families or groups within the community to offer support, in the form of gifts or loans, to help that household meet its food needs when production fails.[42] The reliance on community support as a coping strategy is eroded, however, as a drought persists. The ability of households to assist one another in hard times depends on some households having ties to areas outside of the local community that are not affected by drought.[43] As the adverse conditions broaden to encompass larger areas, the systems of exchange and assistance become insupportable.

Interventions that target the strengthening of community support networks should look to improving complementarity between state and community sponsored social security mechanisms.[44] Assessments can be made of traditional social security systems, and determinations made as to the cost effectiveness of providing state support for these systems rather than attempting a wholesale replacement of community-sponsored with state-sponsored systems. Even in low-income countries, social security can be provided to help the poor cope with food insecurity if effective integration of traditional and national support networks is achieved.[45]

Summary

Vulnerability to food insecurity usually means vulnerability to environmental degradation. Faced with threats to their food security, households may turn to coping strategies that increase immediate income sources and subsistance levels but that have detrimental consequences for the natural environment. Focusing on household coping strategies as an essential part of a decentralized food security monitoring system involves local communities in monitoring efforts and in the design of interventions. NGOs are often in the best position to help coordinate this information gathering and to initiate timely responses.

Interventions that take both household food security and environmental issues into account must consider the short- and long-term trade-offs associated with these dual objectives. Long-term, sustainable, natural resource management initiatives will not be successful if they ignore the short-term food security needs of the local population. Likewise, sustainability will be comprised if long-term environmental concerns are sacrificed for immediate food needs. For sustainable development goals to be achieved, a balance must be struck between these two objectives.

Notes

1. J. Corbett, "Famine and Household Coping Strategies," *World Development* 16, no. 9 (1988): 1009. R. Longhurst, "Household Food Strategies in Response to Seasonality and Famine," *Institute of Development Studies Bulletin* 17 (1986): 27.
2. S. Davies, M. Leach, and R. David, "Food Security and the Environment: Conflict or Complementarity?" *IDS Discussion Paper* (Brighton, England: Institute for Development Studies, University of Sussex, 1991).
3. World Bank, *The Challenge of Hunger in Africa: A Call to Action* (Washington, D. C.: 1986).
4. Davies et al., *IDS Discussion Paper*, 1991.
5. Davies et al., *IDS Discussion Paper*, 1991.
6. Davies et al., *IDS Discussion Paper*, 1991.
7. Corbett, *Famine and Household*, 1988.
8. P. Cutler, "The Response to Drought of Beja Famine Refugees in Sudan," *Disasters* 10, no. 3 (1986). Longhurst, in *IDS Bulletin* 17, 1986. L. M. Malambo, "Rural Food Security in Zambia" (Ph.D. dissertation, Michigan State University, East Lansing, Michigan, (1987). T. E. Downing, "Climatic Variability, Food Security and Smallholder Agriculturalists in Six Districts of Central and Eastern Kenya" Ph.D. dissertation, Clark University, Worcester, Massachusetts, (1988).

9. Corbett, *Famine and Household*, 1988.
10. Longhurst, in *IDS Bulletin*, 1986. M. Watts, *Silent Violence: Food, Famine and Peasantry in Northern Nigeria* (Berkeley: University of California Press, 1983).
11. T. Walker and N. Jodha, "How Small Farm Households Adapt to Risk," in *Crop Insurance for Agricultural Development: Issues and Experience*, eds. P. Hazell, et al. (Baltimore, Maryland: The Johns Hopkins University Press, 1986).
12. Walker and Jodha, in *Crop Insurance*, 1986.
13. Walker and Jodha, in *Crop Insurance*, 1986.
14. Walker and Jodha, in *Crop Insurance*, 1986.
15. Longhurst, in *IDS Bulletin*, 1986. N. Tobert, "The Effect of Drought Among the Zaghawa in Northern Darfu," *Disasters* 9 (1985): 213.
16. Watts, in *Coping with Uncertainty*, 1988.
17. Watts, in *Coping with Uncertainty*, 1988.
18. Watts, in *Coping with Uncertainty*, 1988.
19. Downing, "Climatic Variability," 1988. R. B. Thomas, S. H. B. H. Paine, and B. P. Brenton, "Perspectives on Socio-economic Causes of and Responses to Food Deprivation," *Food and Nutrition Bulletin* 11 (1989): 41.
20. D. C. Mead "Non-farm Income and Food Security: Lessons from Rwanda" in *Household and National Food Security in Southern Africa*, eds. G. D. Mudimu and R. H. Bernstein (Proceedings of the Fourth Annual Conference on Food Security Research in Southern Africa, University of Zimbabwe/Michigan State University Food Security Research Project, Department of Agricultural Economics and Extension, Harare, Zimbabwe, October 31–November 3, 1988), 331. S. M. Swinton, "Drought Survival Tactics of Subsistence Farmers in Niger," *Human Ecology* 16 (1988): 123.
21. Thomas et al., in *Food and Nutrition*, 1989.
22. T. R. Frankenberger, "Production-Consumption Linkages and Coping Strategies at the Household Level" (Paper presented at the Agriculture-Nutrition Linkage Workshop, Bureau of Science and Technology, USAID, Washington, D.C., February 1990).
23. T. R. Frankenberger and D. M. Goldstein, "Food Security, Coping Strategies, and Environmental Degradation," *Arid Lands Newsletter* 30 (1990): 21.
24. Davies et al., *IDS Discussion Paper*, 1991.
25. Davies et al., *IDS Discussion Paper*, 1991.
26. N. S. Jodha, "Poor in Dry Regions of India," *Economic and Political Weekly* 21 no. 27 (1986): 1169.
27. Davies et al., *IDS Discussion Paper*, 1991.
28. D. W. Norman, "Soil Conservation: Using Farming Systems Development as an Aid" (Paper prepared for the Farm Management and Production Economics Service, Agricultural Services Division, Food and Agriculture Organization (FAO), Rome, Italy, 1991).
29. Frankenberger and Goldstein, in *Arid Lands*, 1990.
30. Frankenberger and Goldstein, in *Arid Lands*, 1990.
31. Corbett, *Famine and Household*, 1988. D. J. Campbell and D. D. Trechter,

"Strategies for Coping with Food Consumption Shortage in the Mandora Mountains Region of North Cameroon," *Social Science and Medicine 16* (1982): 2117.

32. J. C. Bryson, J. P. Chudy, and J. M. Pines, *Food for Work: A Review of the 1980s with Recommendations for the 1990s* (Washington, DC: U.S. Agency for International Development, Bureau for Food for Peace and Voluntary Assistance, Office of Program Policy and Management, 1991).

33. Bryson et al., *Food for Work*, 1991.

34. Davies et al., *IDS Discussion Paper*, 1991.

35. Davies et al., *IDS Discussion Paper*, 1991.

36. Davies et al., *IDS Discussion Paper*, 1991.

37. G. R. Conway, "Sustainability in Agricultural Development: Trade-Offs with Productivity, Stability, and Equitability" (Paper presented at the 11th Annual AFRSE Symposium, East Lansing, MI, October 5-10, 1991).

38. Conway, "Sustainability," 1991.

39. R. M. Caldwell, "Land Resource Management in the Sudano-Sahelian Belt of West and Central Africa: A Practical Review" (A draft report prepared for the United Nations Sudano-Sahelian Office, New York, NY, 1991).

40. Davies et al., *IDS Discussion Paper*, 1991.

41. Bryson et al., *Food for Work*, 1991. P. Webb and J. von Braun, *Famine in Ethiopia: Policy Implications of Coping Failure at National and Household Levels* (Washington, DC: International Food Policy Research Institute, 1991).

42. Campbell and Trechter, in *Social Science*, 1982.

43. Thomas et al., in *Food and Nutrition*, 1989.

44. J. von Braun, "Social Security in Sub-Saharan Africa: Reflections on Policy Challenges," in *Social Security in Developing Countries*, eds. E. Ahmad, J. Dreze, J. Hills, and A. Sen (Oxford: Oxford University Press, 1991), 395.

45. For examples of interventions that have targeted state and community sponsored social security mechanisms, see E. Ahmad, "Social Security and the Poor: Choices for Developing Countries," *The World Bank Research Observer 6, no. 1* (1991): 105.

CHAPTER SEVEN

PRIVATE SECTOR INITIATIVES FOR SUSTAINABLE DEVELOPMENT
A Better Approach

Richard S. Gordon and Antonio Calzada-Rovirosa

Dick Gordon and Antonio Calzada-Rovirosa, both of Arizona State University's School of Agribusiness and Environmental Resources, present a private sector perspective on efforts to strengthen food security through environmental conservation that relies heavily of financial cost-benefit analysis. They raise questions: how are we going to afford a much needed global cleanup of waterways, land and air, and stimulate food production to ease world hunger? Who will pay the bills? How do we make good economic choices, and what is best left to private initiative? It is interesting to note that as Gordon and Calzada attempt to answer these questions, they find themselves at the same starting point as DeWitt, Martin, Clay, Vaughn, Flores and Frankenberger: people-centered development and human transformation.

UNTIL QUITE RECENTLY, MOST DEVELOPING country governments and international nongovernmental organizations (NGOs), as well as many agencies of industrialized nation governments (particularly the United States), regarded private initiative and investment by Western firms in developing countries as suspect. However, by 1982 this attitude had shifted, and economic development increasingly was seen as the result of successful business formation by many firms of quite different types, outlooks and areas of expertise. This was in contrast to the former belief that economic development could be created "top down" by government through central planning and establishing state-run industries and parastatal marketing organizations.

Now, profit motivated entrepreneurs, marketing middlemen, and multinational firms, previously considered part of the problem of underdevelopment, are being sought as investors and partners to help revitalize tired or hamstrung economies through private sector investment and export development. The economic role of national, state and provincial governments worldwide is increasingly being seen as one that facilitates private sector economic growth through policy reforms and incentives. What has transpired over the past decade or two to cause such a shift in attitude?

1. By the early 1980s it was clear that, overall, very large governmental organizations in many developing countries, as well as the smaller parastatal organizations, were not developing viable economies that were environmentally sustainable, particularly with respect to food production, processing, storage, distribution and marketing. There were too many examples of new bureaucracies creating new barriers, and of employees looking to these development organizations for employment, rather than for the mission of developing their country.[1]

2. The former colonial powers, (Germany, Belgium, Holland, France, and Great Britain, and later Japan), were purchasing an increasing percentage of the raw agricultural production of developing countries, usually for shipment "home", to be followed by value-added processing and marketing by firms in the developed country whence it came. In the last year for which figures are available, Germany, Holland, and Japan marketed over 50 percent of the world's value-added food products, the United States only 6 percent, and any individual developing country only a negligible amount. In a sense, the Germans, Dutch and Japanese were harvesting some thirty years of foreign assistance investment in production technology in these developing countries.

3. The globalization of world food trade was essentially completed by the middle of the past decade. Those products best fitted for a particular market in terms of cost and quality displaced older, so-called commodity products no matter where produced. Consequently, it finally dawned on U.S. and other authorities that the focus was now on markets and marketing; as in finding and reaching customers, financing trade and the distribution and upgrading of basic crops, etc. Clearly, government organizations were not designed to be marketeers, purveyors, processors, and so forth.

4. Recent American emphasis on private initiative and volunteerism and the disintegration of the former Soviet and East European centralized economies has had enormous impact. The United States now is encouraging investment in Russia and Central Europe as well as offering considerable grant money to NGOs, universities, even private firms, to aid in the privatization process and a shift to market driven economies.

This is not the place to debate whether such policies are good or bad, only to say that economic necessities, the political climate and globalization of trade have come together so that developing country priorities, often responding to donor government pressure, now reflect a radical increase in the latitude given private citizens, NGOs, firms, and even capital.

Accordingly, we in Northern countries must ask ourselves, our governments, and our international donor institutions whether current enthusiasm for private investment, deal making, and market economy oriented programs will wind up as discredited as former government managed programs have been, this time through fraud and exploitation of the people and the land.

Clearly there are new issues, new problems to be faced by all parties, particularly nongovernmental organizations (NGOs), and in the forefront is one general issue: that of environmental sustainability. In terms of food production, environmental sustainability means the ability to produce crops or livestock over the long term without damaging or using up the natural resource that supports such production. To address this issue one must consciously add an environmental management component to any long-term agricultural or other economic development plan.

The production orientation of older international development programs did much to obscure our consideration of alternatives, particularly those that looked at market need and worked backwards, through finance and processing to the production technology required to meet the need. In addition, preserving, even strengthening, the resource upon which production depends is crucial. There is a new style of environmental activism that has taken advantage of market forces. It has, for example, developed an environmentally sustainable approach to preserving the Brazilian rainforest in a way that makes economic sense and is people-centered: turning colonizers into conservationists who harvest and sell renewable forest extracts (see Chapter Three).

Further, the fight to save the rainforest highlights a key issue: economically deprived people need to feed themselves and their families now. They are not interested in the long-term consequences of their production practices if they are not going to be alive anyway. Increasingly, they rightly point to what industrialized nations have done to the earth's land and water and link overconsumption in the North with global environmental degradation. Industrialized nations use over 75 percent of the world's resources for a declining fraction of the world's population (estimated to be some 20 percent or so). We are challenged by our friends in these developing countries to answer the question, "Is the industrialized world's stewardship of our planet something that one points to with pride? Is it to be emulated?" We know the answer: NO!

It is also clear that environmental considerations will have to be built into the cost of every project that governments and private enterprises undertake. Concomitantly, environmental programs will have to be economically justified as part of any development or investment proposal.

For example, how does one pay for a major reforestation project? Raise taxes on the citizens in the region affected? Or develop a scheme by which the forest will throw off enough income to pay for its establishment and maintenance? Timbering? Harvesting nuts? How about cleaning up waterways without increasing the cost of drinking water? How does one calculate an economic return for a public expenditure? How does a poor country pay for preservation of a critical resource, or shutdown of a major polluter that is a significant employer? How will Eastern Europe pay to clean up after the destruction of draconian Soviet industrial policy? The economic catastrophe that will result from closing down facilities that are the main source of both pollution and employment for towns and villages is almost too great to contemplate. Even in the United States, some claim that newer laws and requirements for toxic waste cleanup will almost certainly impoverish some communities. Some claim that the United States seems to have adopted Soviet style rules rather than guidelines and policies that free people to use their own ingenuity for cleanup. If we continue to encourage hysteria over potential harm so that we totally lose sight of the situation, we are likely to render significant parts of our economy non-competitive with similar economies in other parts of the world.

Clearly these are explosive issues. Most of our colleagues in Third World countries see little sense in what they perceive as an overexaggerated concern in America for safety and potential harm compared to the problems they face:[2] inadequate food, particularly for high-risk populations of pregnant women and children; inadequate shelter, lack of preventative health care, and lack of access to schooling.

These same colleagues all want to see dramatic stimulation of economic development in their countries, particularly of food production, sustainable over the long term. They feel that small changes in ground water or soil fertility are an acceptable price to pay for more food, provided such changes are ultimately reversible and do not have a direct impact on human health. But what is *new* is that Third World colleagues now believe that nongovernmental initiatives need to be taken and new ties forged between growers and local and foreign firms to process, store, distribute and market good quality food.

Successful manufacturing companies in industrialized nations are always searching for better sources of raw material that can be locally harvested and processed to preserve quality before being exported or even sold locally. Yet, the statist laws of too many developing countries prevent direct investment by, or a reasonable basis for repayment of investment to, the foreign partner, as well as blocking the ability of the foreign participant to make a reasonable profit based on the element of risk involved. Until the 1980s, many developing countries had laws that made it very difficult for a venture to operate when it involved a local entity, such as a grower, and a foreign party. Now, country after country is changing its laws to stimulate private initiatives and consequently development. Why is that? Are we comfortable with the way such matters are changing?

What Is Meant by Private Initiative?

What kind of private initiative are we talking about that stimulates food production and other development both in an economic and environmentally sustainable fashion? Crucial to understanding what follows is acceptance of the idea that a key purpose of government and government agencies is to promote trade, set ground rules for commerce and ensure that equitable conditions for business exist with other nations. However, the primary role of government is not itself to enter into trade and business. Creating economic development really means generating new sources of revenue, and investing in and receiving the return from new resources and enterprises. Staying within the confines of the old order leads to increasing taxation to pay for more and more services. Meanwhile, the "economy" (the net sum of exchange of goods and services), instead of being nurtured, is further and further circumscribed; the outcome is predictably depressing.

Private and Nongovernmental Sector Initiatives

Lack of hard currency is the greatest barrier to sustainable development for developing nations from Africa to Eastern Europe. Economic development in virtually all regions of the world requires some inputs external to the local setting. Further, to sustain development over the long term, a continuous flow of external inputs is usually required, paid for by some of the proceeds from previous enterprises or foreign loans. Clearly, if development is funded only by debt, the burden gets unmanageable, as we have seen in Latin America.

Private sector initiatives for development enterprises avoid all nonfinancial arguments used to justify the cost of their use, such as parks, forests, wetlands, and wildlife areas. They require proponents and participants to stand on their own feet and defend the worth, cost and returns of a very specific enterprise or undertaking. The taxes on the venture and its employees become the "reward" or return garnered by the state.

For example, managers of American forests are torn between the different agendas of the forests' various users: recreationers, conservationists, loggers, and ranchers. If their tax base continues to erode, they have to find some fair means to sustain the forests over time. Controlled logging or cattle grazing can be used in a manner to provide fee income and to help keep the forest in shape to serve multiple agendas. In the United States, while all eyes are on public lands, we should not forget the enormous acreage that companies such as Weyerhauser maintain. Forest development is planned over four to six decades. This is not something a new firm in a developing country can do overnight without outside help.

Because they do not require the official blessing or approval of the state, private initiatives themselves assume the risk of failure, and all that entails. An investment or financial community then can evaluate risk in funding the venture based on:

1. the amount of return the investor must have (if an ownership or equity share is obtained); or
2. the interest rate that must be charged if money is advanced as a loan.

The ideal role of government is to establish the rules under which private initiative is to function. This includes fiscal policy, environmental policy, size of company or market share until antimonopoly rules come into play, and percentage of foreign ownership. As mentioned above, some governments block development through limitations on some of these matters, such as foreign investment in (or ownership of) an enterprise, export rules, import duties, extension of credit from the country's central bank (even when backed by an international body such as the World Bank), and so forth. While many of these rules were put in place to guard small countries against what was regarded as undue capitalistic exploitation by the large nations, today they are largely counterproductive. Let us now examine what is productive.

Business Incubators

With the fading of direct opposition to private sector initiative in national development activities has come the growth of a new strategy now spreading around the world: business innovation and incubation programs that lead to the kind of family income generation that can guarantee food security.

The term "business incubator" generally refers to multitenant facilities established to house and assist new business ventures in order to increase their chances of being successful. Business incubators are not stand-alone institutions. Where they have been most successful, they are outgrowths of regional economic development programs and strategies. These, in turn, are the result of cooperation and support from state and local governments, private sector firms, nonprofit organizations, colleges and universities.

In short, the incubator picks up where the government leaves off, becoming the focus of a regional support network designed to stimulate economic development without requiring government approval or even decision making. The subject of business incubators is complex and lengthy. Following are the highlights of what they provide:

Affordable work space on flexible terms. Landlords of industrial and commercial property generally seek long-term lease commitments and financially stable tenants. Incubators allow new firms to rent only the space they need on flexible terms such as month-to-month leases, thus freeing up cash needed for equipment and operating capital during the early phases of a new venture.

Financial assistance. Most entrepreneurs lack sufficient seed and operating capital to launch ventures and operate them until they become investable, if not profitable. Few investors will take a chance on new and unproven companies. Most successful incubators become expert in managing seed and startup capital as part of the incubator, freeing the entrepreneur to get on with his business development.

Professional business assistance. Management errors are a major cause of new business failures. Many entrepreneurs starting new businesses lack sufficient business management training and experience. The manager of an incubator, housing and overseeing a number of ventures, provides onsite assistance to the tenants, usually quite informally. The incubator manager also serves as a key link to connecting each venture to a larger network of financial institutions, investors, government programs, and professionals who may be able to help a specific enterprise with a specific problem. The result is almost continuous support and on-the-job management training.

Shared office services and facilities. Stand-alone startup ventures face high initial rates of overhead. In incubators you can share a xerox machine, telephone receptionist, computers, etc. It is amazing how much one saves when office services, engineering support, and machinery are shared.

The United States Agency for International Development (USAID) is currently funding a study of the use of incubators in developing countries. New strategies and specific tactics are being developed to facilitate nongovernmental, private initiative with respect to long-term sustainable development. Many of these incubators will house agribusinesses.

Joint Ventures

Private initiatives for economic development, particularly enterprises that produce, process, store, distribute and market food in developing countries, often can best accomplish their purpose via a joint venture with a foreign partner. The foreign partner supplies some technology and has access to export markets for products from the joint enterprise. In country processing near the site of crop production increases local jobs and is the best method of ensuring high-quality production. The joint venture purchases from nearby producers. Except for agronomic demonstration purposes, the joint venture rarely owns more land than required for its plant. Leasing land is a preferred strategy. The enterprise partners work out some means of sharing investment and profit, of managing the venture and overseeing its personnel, of pointing output towards domestic or exportmarkets or both. It makes for a much healthier relationship if the developing country partner arranges for financing for its share of the joint venture, rather than asking the foreign partner to stand all the cost and, therefore, all the risk. Following are some important questions to ask in setting up a joint venture:

- Can the enterprise procure enough material from enough growers to get reasonably reliable and uniform supplies of good quality produce?
- Will the growers be amenable to forming some form of collective or cooperative to afford the cost of larger capital items, such as tractors and harvesters?
- Will the growers share in the returns from export sales, particularly if they will accept technical direction from the enterprise?
- What will in country laws permit, if growers do come together as a production cooperative? Should they have some ownership in the processing venture?

Ordinarily a Western processing/marketing venture partner will care less about its share of equity than its control of venture responsibilities. Most will want to manage the venture if they are going to introduce their technology and market the output under their name. Yet there are still more than a few developing countries that will not permit such management arrangements. Nevertheless, discussing who owns what share or percentage of the enterprise leads to some very interesting negotiations.

For example, negotiating private equity joint venture initiatives with the Chinese can be very slow. Chinese authorities want to make sure that contributions of all parties are precisely enumerated to share profits proportionally. However, this poses the problem of putting meaningful price tags on apples and oranges. For example: How many workers are equivalent to one power shovel? When the concept of a contractual agreement was introduced in China, it permitted partners to agree on how to split profits without respect to contributions. This is an important principle, because how do you value the land or the ocean that supplies the agricultural raw material for the venture? Realistically, there is no way. While profit splits in contractual ventures roughly follow new capital contributions, the foreign partner brings his past experience and access to technology and markets to match the natural resource base of the developing country partner.

The goal of private initiatives, whether or not there is a foreign partner, is to have an enterprise operate within the laws of the developing country but otherwise be free of interference in its day-to-day operations. This should build reliance on the individual ingenuity of the enterprise managers. They will quickly learn how to anticipate problems and how to respond to unexpected situations without having to clear everything through several bureaucratic layers. Private initiative means turning the focus away from learning how to manipulate or get around bureaucracy and its rules to dealing with the real, operational questions at hand.

In sustainable economic development, sustainable implies the following:

- The enterprise generates more net revenue than it requires to stay in operation. It has to build facilities and process raw materials. It has to furnish a return to those who funded it so that they will continue their interest in that location. Finally, it has to pay taxes to the country that housed the enterprise, and supplied infrastructure and people, so that development by others can proceed.
- The enterprise places no unusual burdens on its surrounding environment or on the region in which it operates. This means building into any operation the same requirements regarding worker safety, environmental pollution control and product quality control as one practices in the home country of the investor.

By way of an example, we can look at what it might take to move the peasants, or *campesinos*, on communal farms in Mexico beyond their general state of controlled poverty. This would be not only for their benefit, but also to increase total food production in Mexico.

Privatizing Agriculture and Increasing Food Production in Mexico

With respect to food production, land reform is one of the most troubling issues. Typically, former state owned or public lands are reapportioned to the peasantry in small lots, five to ten acres. There are very few plant or animal crops and little technology or credit that can sustain any kind of farming on plots that small. Nevertheless, whether in Bulgaria or Mexico, the populist approach to giving land back to the people blinds the politician to the economic realities.

Through the agrarian reform brought about by the Revolution of 1910, Mexico divided its huge land holdings into private farms and *ejidos*. An *ejido* is a community that receives the use of land without ownership. The worker's right to use the land is attested to by land Agrarian Certificates. Workers *(campesinos)* receiving individual parcels are called *ejidotarios*. While the original parcels were somewhat larger, the land in an *ejido* is currently divided into some twenty to thirty parcels of three to five hectares each. After eighty years of land distribution and redistribution, *ejido* plots have shrunk in size because the children of an individual *campesino* or *ejidotario* have the right to inherit the use of the plot, thus subdividing the original parcel. While the individual *campesino* or *ejidotario* has usufruct rights to the land, he cannot buy or sell it, nor can he use it as collateral for a loan.

The *ejido* is governed by a council, usually associated with one specific location or village. The elders of the village tend also to be in control of the *ejido* council. Because the amount of each parcel is so small, and the economic value of the crop produced is limited, obtaining credit for seed, fertilizer and equipment is difficult for the average person.

We have made a fairly detailed study of land reform in Mexico and conclude that over the past eighty years the Mexican authorities have focused on land distribution rather than on stimulating and improving production. The different regimes seemed to assume that by giving farm laborers access to land, increased production automatically would follow. Consequently, although every Mexican regime continues to promise new land distribution, central governmental authorities only recently have recognized that technical assistance and agricultural credits are required. Such are needed if Mexico is to lift the *ejidotario* out of poverty and increase food exports to the new global markets.

Under current law, the *campesino* has been given priority as a credit recipient. The banks have been directed by the government to lend on the collateral value of the crop to be produced. However, an elaborate loan application process and the marginal nature of his collateral greatly diminish the individual *ejidotario's* chance of obtaining credit. Accordingly, most agricultural loans are made to private farmers who usually have larger holdings and can pledge their land as collateral. The banks rightly regard such loans as lower risks than loans to individual *ejidotarios*.

Consequently, commercial banks associated with Mexico's Banrural system (those charged with making agricultural loans for *ejido* production) will not lend amounts higher than the minimum level required by the Mexican government for *ejido* loans. The result is that what is lent to an individual farmer for his plot in an *ejido* is not sufficient to improve the land and its yield over time. An additional negative, from the bank's point of view, is that the marginal nature of the loan leads to numerous loan defaults. The nature of the collateral pledged usually leaves the banks empty-handed.

The Mexican Secretariat of Agriculture and Water Resources (SARH) has offered technical assistance for *campesinos* in the last twenty years through classroom training and practical production support. Regardless of the type of training, even today only a few *ejidos* are commercially viable. It appears that the successful *campesinos* are those who previously worked as laborers on private (usually larger) farms and learned efficient production practices. Matters got so bad that by 1988 the SARH offered assistance to the *campesinos* by supplying managers to each interested *ejido*. These managers took charge, organized collective production and gave direct orders to each farm worker. This was done instead of training *ejidotarios* in effective production practices, paying no attention to whether or not the individual had any previous agricultural production experience. Authoritarian management plus administrative absenteeism (bureaucrats are not too interested in working out in the boonies) only further depressed the *campesino's* economic condition. Consequently, many *campesino-ejidotarios* who received agricultural loans were forced to sell their personal belongings to cover existing debts.

From this experience, a few far-seeing *ejidos* took a page from Mexico's book of successful cooperatives, which include Ocean Gardens and Conasupo, and regrouped as an operating production collective. They recruited professionals as managers, who understood they were working for the *ejido*, not a government agency. As a result, production improved and the full-time manager trained the *campesinos* in efficient farming practices. Although this recourse to private administrative initiatives did improve production for the few who took this step, still all *ejidos* remain terribly hampered by their inability to pledge the land as collateral and by the excessive paperwork required to make a loan application. Such barriers irrefutably discourage individual and group initiatives.

About 90 percent of the paperwork each individual *campesino-ejidotario* now submits could be eliminated if the government permitted each individual *ejido* to organize as a private cooperative without otherwise changing its fundamental nature or structure. The individual no longer would have to deal with a slow and often sullen bureaucrat in order to get his or her agrarian permit (showing that he or she has the right to use the land) before he or she can obtain the necessary bank credit. If the *ejido* were a private cooperative with legal ownership of the land, such paperwork could be done collectively, and there could be an administrative person trained to deal with credit and other formalities.

Organizing as a cooperative still leaves the troubling question of using *ejido* land for collateral: If the *ejido* is not able to pay the loan back after two successive years, what then? Instead of the bank having the right to take possession of the land, we are recommending to appropriate Mexican authorities that the *ejido* be required to hire a farm manager, mutually acceptable to the bank and the *ejido*. This person would take charge of the collective, being sensitive to the feelings of the *ejido* council. He would train the workers and establish meaningful farming operations. Not only would this give the banks a chance to recover their loans, but a revitalized *ejido* could agglomerate additional hectares for production to which the members agree. Under such circumstances, well-managed *ejidos* could become net exporters of food to the surrounding region.

Unfortunately the present Mexican regime only has two more years in office. If it does not make such changes very soon, people, particularly in the remote rural areas, will take matters into their own hands. Mexican newspapers are full of stories of growing numbers of *campesinos* and *ejido* councils demanding that *ejidos* be eliminated, converting to a format similar to what we have suggested. No matter what is done, failure to respond to Mexico's need for continuing agrarian reform or to harness local initiative will perpetuate poverty for over 41 million people. Further, food production will continue to fall far short of what is needed for Mexico's domestic consumption, let alone for export.

This example illustrates how a government, with very good intentions, gets in the way of achieving its own objectives, and how private sector initiatives can achieve both individual and government objectives. With a few simple changes in the current law, Mexico could convert the *ejidos* into private cooperatives so that the present fragmented land parcels are worked as a unit. At the same time, if the *ejidos* were permitted to pledge their land as collateral, any change in the law would have to specify what happens in case of loan default. A provision that the bank could not take the land provided the *ejido* hired management until it was profitable would suffice. With such changes, Mexican food production would increase quite rapidly.

Notes

1. This is reviewed in great detail in *Daedulus* 118 (1989): 1.
2. With the world of analytical instrumentation improving by orders of magnitude each decade, "zero" becomes a detectable level, and what previously was thought to be perfectly safe or sustainable, suddenly has to be cleaned up, usually at enormous expense. This cleanup is based on methods proscribed by a third party such as a regulatory agency. One unintended consequence is that such action often forces operating firms to move offshore, particularly when they are convinced that their environmental discharge causes negligible harm to man and the ecosphere. Another country will welcome them for economic reasons.

CHAPTER EIGHT

FOOD, FAMILY, GOD AND EARTH
Compete for the Whole

Frances Spivy-Weber

Frances Spivy-Weber, national chairperson of the U.S. Citizens Network on the United Nations Conference on Environment and Development, and a director of The National Audubon Society, lived out of a suitcase for much of 1991 to carry a call to citizen participation across the country and around the globe. Yet her message to our symposium, at the end of the year, was as fresh as it was pertinent: compete for wholeness in your personal life, community and world. Don't let a quest for conservation, or for food security, or for cost effectiveness reduce you to tunnel vision. Compete for completeness and join hands in the journey.

THE SUCCESS OF A CITIZENS' movement for sustainable development draws strength from indigenous people and their philosophies. It depends on people like you, and on people like me.

A Navajo participant in the United Nations Conference on Environment and Development (UNCED), also called the "Earth Summit," described to me the organizing principle for his life and village. He drew a circle that was balanced on one axis by spiritual and family concerns, and on the other axis by nature and economics (or livelihood). When these four priorities—God, family, the environment, and bread winning—are not in balance, there is no circle.

These are the priorities that delegates to the Earth Summit in Rio de Janeiro are investigating as they look at what can be done to restore the environment. These are elements we must look to far beyond Rio. These four elements represent personal ideals that we as world citizens can examine within ourselves and our own villages. What are our personal priorities? What personal philosophies govern the way we live? What can our towns, villages, or tribes do to improve the environment? How do we organize the way in which we live locally, nationally, and globally to protect the environment?

The Earth Summit officially began in December 1989 with a resolution in the United Nations General Assembly. It officially ends June 12, 1992, in Rio de Janeiro, Brazil. But as a process, it must continue beyond June 1992. We must continually check and recheck our priorities.

Looking at my own country, the United States of America, I feel we are out of balance. Our circle is tilted heavily toward livelihood. That is not a bad priority, but it is only one of four. Americans should put into our national, local, and personal priorities more emphasis on nature, family, and spiritual values.

Many people and communities today are reevaluating their lifestyles. They are starting to recycle. They are paying attention to what they eat. They are engaging in activities that are easier on the Earth and its natural resources. They are speaking more forcefully to politicians, but not forcefully enough.

Towns are becoming an extremely important voice. A town in Florida provides a good example of what I am talking about. This town's people annually evaluate a specific set of criteria that they agreed would measure their quality of life. Depending upon the outcome of the annual evaluation, adjustments are made in local policies. The town also works to create ways of making adjustments in state and federal policies that improve on those measurable criteria.

Another town, Arcadia, California, became split after the Gulf War last year. The split was so pronounced that they could no longer agree on even local issues. They secured donated time on public television and engaged in a three-hour dispute resolution. They started working out their problems on television, a unique use of modern resources to engage people in thinking about how to live and how to set priorities nationally, locally and personally.

Now, what does all this have to do with global conferences on environment and development? The Earth Summit is not a conference of the United Nations and governments deciding what we should do. It is a conference of governments and the United Nations asking people like you and me what we and they should do. And, quite frankly, we are not expressing our views as clearly and as massively as we can.

The United Nations has opened up its process more than ever before to participation of organizations. It is relatively easy to become accredited to participate in the debate. The only limiting factor is space. But, as in the example of Arcadia, California, we live in an era of modern technology. Through television and telecommunications, organizations who want to participate can do so. Our only limitations are ingenuity, occasionally money, and a willingness to roll up our sleeves and get to work to help create a new kind of world.

One of the issues that UNCED will address is energy. Governments are saying what they are willing to do on energy policy issues. But they need to hear from you. Your organization can pass resolutions and send them to your head of state, parliament or Congress, and the government bodies of your organizations. You can ask colleagues in your sector or your local region to do similar things. Speak out on what you believe is sound energy policy. If you and everyone like you in every other region of the world speaks out, we will get much closer to securing the energy policy *we* want, not what the politicians think we want.

The Earth Summit provides a similar opportunity for action on each and every issue you, the reader, are working on: food security, agriculture, biological diversity, water quality or quantity, poverty, and dozens more. No matter what the issue, there will be a path for information and your position to get into the debate at UNCED and into working groups beyond. That path starts locally. It starts right now.

Our collective political voice is extremely powerful. Many of the contributors to and readers of this volume work on development issues. You are a powerful lobby. I work for Audubon, and Audubon and many of the other environmental groups represented in this volume are a tremendously powerful political lobby. Some contributors and readers are from business. Your economic clout makes you a very powerful political lobby. And some represent churches and other religious groups. You are an extremely important moral lobby.

Our success in creating the world in which we want to live will be in pulling these voices together to talk about the same things. We will each approach these issues from different perspectives. But we should not try to say that hunger, nature, economics, or spiritual values is the most important thing. We should be taking advice from the Navajo I spoke of earlier. We must bring all of these ideals into our circle. We should not compete to be first. We should compete to be whole. And you can use UNCED as a starting point to bring that whole together.

AFTERWORD

Katie Smith

MIDWAY THROUGH "GROWING OUR FUTURE," we received a jolting reminder that the world's most complex problems are right next door: in the midst of a discussion of human rights in the Horn of Africa in Cultural Survival's case study group, Vernon Masayesva, Chairman of America's Hopi Tribe, told us about a struggle his people were having in northern Arizona to restructure age-old mining accords that were endangering waterways on their land. A significant problem, he admitted, was that the Hopi's quest for social justice would have an impact on the human rights of neighboring Navajo people. Resource wars are rife throughout the world. It is only by providing poor people and indigenous peoples like the Hopi with the tools needed for leverage in peaceful negotiations—education, opportunities to generate income (for example, jobs and markets), a place in our justice system and a listening ear, that we avert conflict resolution via war and bloodshed. Such conflict plagues the world's poorest countries, and is the ultimate menace to food security and the environment.

At the close of "Growing Our Future," a Phoenix lawyer, George Paul, cautioned conference participants that the next twenty years may be the most important in the life of the planet. He was right to underscore that we are facing a brink, but it is certainly not the first. We don't have to look too far back to find humankind on the brink of nuclear destruction, or in a "war to end all wars," scourged by disease, or drowned in a great flood. There have been and will be many brinks. So far, the planet has survived, civilizations have perished. The lives truly at stake are our own and our children's. So what will we do? Shore up the brink? Or scamper headlong over like lemmings? Build an ark? Or wait absentmindedly for the floods?

Eighteenth-century historian Edward Gibbon noted the link between citizens' failure to serve the commonweal and society's disintegration in his analysis of the demise of Athens in *The Decline and Fall of the Roman Empire:*

> When the Athenians finally wanted not to give to society but for society to give to them, when the freedom they wished for most was freedom from responsibility, then Athens ceased to be free.

On one level, the Earth Summit process has been about combatting world hunger and conserving environment, but on its most basic level, it is asking each of us to examine our motivations, the values they engender and actions they generate. Are our lives coherent? Do we exemplify the integrity of creation in our own and our families' pursuits? Only by competing for a balanced whole in our own microenvironment, by starting with ourselves and by serving others, will we ever make a difference for the world.

APPENDIX I

CASES

CASE ONE

TUAREG REHABILITATION PROJECT

Frank G. Cookingham
World Vision

WORLD VISION BEGAN PROJECT WORK in the south of Mali in 1982. The
severe drought in 1983 to 1985 led to a major relief effort in the
country's northernmost district, or "seventh region." In 1987 to 1988
programming was shifted from direct relief to more developmental
activities. The Menaka Oases Program is located in Menaka Circle,
which is a pastoral zone populated by Tamasheq-speaking nomadic
groups (Tuaregs and Dahousahaqs). There are only two towns of
significant size, Menaka (5,000 people) and Anderamboukane (1,500
people).

Pasture is the prime natural resource in the seventh region. The
most rational use of the pasture is through a mobile lifestyle that
allows the herder to move his animals about to the best grazing areas
in cyclical patterns. This avoids the overuse and degradation of the
land that occurs when herders become sedentary.

The purpose of the Menaka Oases Program development strategy
is to help nomadic groups develop new ways of thinking and behavior that will increase the likelihood of sustaining the essence of their
way of life in a difficult and changing environment. Program interventions are designed to secure points of refuge for the nomads to buffer
the devastating effects of arid years.

Lessons Learned

This list of lessons learned was developed from a World Vision
program evaluation report on World Vision's work in Menaka.[1]
- *Enhancement of the resource base at each oasis site is as much a
  spiritual activity as it is a physical one, for each step toward*

*alleviating the adverse effects of environmental degradation in-
spires hope for the future.*

A major component of the World Vision program is reestablishing
and enhancing the natural resource base at thirty-five oasis sites. The
purpose is to provide environmental safety nets at oasis sites in times
of drought. It is not intended that the oasis sites become places for
sedentary groups.

There are four major activities that occur in different combinations
at the sites: pasture and agricultural land regeneration, water supply
development, agricultural training and gardening, and forestry. Interventions are designed to be carried out during the dry season when
nomads are near the oasis sites. Implementations are planned by the
communities, and avoid use of complex techniques or expensive
equipment.

- *Perceptions of the appropriateness of technology influence programming effectiveness.*

Use of appropriate technology is especially important in trying to
help nomads adopt new agricultural practices. This was illustrated
during a visit to Tinebout, located along a lake, where an experimental
rice paddy had been abandoned after two years of experimentation.
The paddy had been irrigated by using a diesel pump provided by a
French sister city. There were many problems encountered with maintaining the pump. Given the remote location, providing fuel and spare
parts and repair services was difficult. Given the conditions, reliable
irrigation was essential to cultivate rice.

The nomads who worked in the paddy, skeptical about the chances
that the paddy would produce adequate grain on a reliable basis,
especially with the pump acting erratically, eventually refused to continue working. In retrospect, even with practical reliable technology
for irrigation it would have been difficult for the nomads to overcome
their reluctance to engage in agriculture. The inappropriate technology doomed the experiment to failure.

- *Small scale enterprises can stimulate changes in behavior to protect the environment.*

Before the drought of 1984 to 1985, there were no permanent
houses within Menaka Circle outside Menaka and Anderamboukane
and four neighborhood villages. As people settled around oasis sites
to survive, they began building permanent wooden houses, which
threatens the trees that survived the drought.

Four models for woodless construction have been adapted to the nomadic setting in the World Vision program. Each is designed to be built of mud bricks with locally fabricated tools. They are intended to be affordable, aesthetically appealing, and technically appropriate. A total of thirty-five masons have been trained to build the simple igloo, while five other masons have been trained to build more complex structures. Four of these masons have successfully built woodless structures while using standard contracting methods.

- *Both community participation and government participation are essential for effective programming.*

Extensive research and analysis by Sahelian experts has produced a plausible and even probable "trend scenario" of increased dependence on Western countries and relatively rapid erosion of regional natural resources.[2] More positive scenarios can materialize only through a complex set of interactions of Sahelian governments, rural communities, and city dwellers; changes in social roles and structures; changes in national policies; and changes in external assistance by foreign governments and NGOs. There is no simple way forward to a better future for the Sahel. What is needed is a more profound transformation of the way in which the various relationships are structured.

Dialogue with communities is the basis for identifying potential interventions in the World Vision program. Community members trained as animators seek to assure the active participation of the population before permitting technical teams to initiate project interventions. Each community is encouraged to articulate its problems and explore possible solutions.

Project interventions are directed by oasis community councils. The council is responsible for the collection of all community project resources: cash, labor, and in-kind reimbursements.

Submission and endorsement of a project concept document is a prerequisite for all major program activities at an oasis site. The document is based on community discussions about the purpose of an intervention, the resources that will be needed, action steps and schedules, and roles and responsibilities. It must be endorsed by the oasis council and government development committees at neighborhood and Circle levels. There is a serious effort to involve local government authorities and services in all program activities. The World Vision program serves to increase the contact between the nomad chiefs and the local government authorities.

- *Food resources can be programmed effectively as inputs in development activities.*

The Menaka program has employed food resources in a number of purposes and roles. Food resources served as seed capital in the barter of food commodities for animals that were loaned to families to replenish their herds, and as income transfer when they were given to families who had received a small herd. The purpose was to limit the risk that the family would have to sell the newly acquired animals to feed themselves.

Tree planting, tree care, and wild grass seeding are new technologies to herders. These interventions benefit the community at large, over a longer period of time, but there is little direct immediate benefit to the persons actually performing the task. It is unlikely that herders will experiment with them unless there is some incentive. Food resources were used as a full-wage payment to elicit participation from the community in trying these technologies.

Recession sorghum and vegetable gardens were other new technologies that provided some direct benefit to the participant herders in the form of crops. A partial wage payment in food commodities was provided as a participation incentive. The food resources were very effective with poorer families; they were able to purchase some animals toward replenishing their herds.

Notes

1. Frank G. Cookingham, "Evaluation Report: Menaka Oases Program, Mali Seventh Region" (Monrovia, California: World Vision International, February 1990).
2. Organization for Economic Cooperation and Development, *The Sahel Facing the Future: Increasing Dependence or Structural Transformation* (Paris: Organization for Economic Cooperation and Development, 1988).

INTEGRATED CONSERVATION AND DEVELOPMENT
Sierra de las Minas Biosphere Reserve, Guatemala

Bradley L. Ack, World Wildlife Fund
Andreas Lehnhoff, Defensores de la Naturaleza

THIS PROJECT BEGAN IN 1989 with the goal of developing a Biosphere Reserve in the Sierra de las Minas region of Guatemala, to be followed by the design and implementation of an integrated program linking community-based, environmentally sound development with the protection of biological diversity and management of natural resources in the area. While this particular project is a relatively new experience, its design embodies much of the learning of the past six years of World Wildlife Fund's Wildlands and Human Needs Program in designing, developing, and managing integrated conservation and development projects (ICDPs).

Background

The Sierra de las Minas Biosphere Reserve lies in northeastern Guatemala, with an area of approximately 250 square kilometers of rugged mountainous terrain encompassing seven life zones and species-rich cloud forests. Numerous rare and endangered plants and animals such as the quetzal, jaguar, possibly the harpy eagle, tapir, white monk orchid and high numbers of endemic plants and invertebrates are found here.

The area is naturally divided both by topography and access into three distinct zones that lie on three sides of the Sierra. The northern zone (the Polochic River valley) is inhabited primarily by subsistence farming Kekchi Indians on the lower slopes of the Sierra, with large plantation agriculture in the valley below. The western zone of Chilasco is a high plain area abutted by cloud forest and dominated by subsistence agriculture and intensive vegetable production. The southern side of the Sierra (the Motagua River valley), is populated primarily by *ladinos* (non-Indian hispanics) with higher population densities, more industrial development, and with plantation food production in the valley below.

There are more than 100 settlements in and around the Sierra and many thousands of people depend on its natural resources. In addition, as the last extensive montane forest in this region of Guatemala, it plays an extremely important role in producing and safeguarding the vital water supply for the communities in the valleys below.

The area has come under increasing threat in recent years due primarily to large timber companies vying for access to the extensive timber resources it houses. Construction of a paper pulp plant in the Motagua Valley also poses a threat to the Sierra. In addition, both continuing increasing conversion of forested lands to agricultural production and expansion of hunting in the high mountain areas have increased pressure on the Sierra de las Minas ecosystem.

World Wildlife Fund (WWF) involvement in this project began in early 1989 after the government of Guatemala passed legislation establishing the National Protected Areas Council and defining forty-four priority wildlands to be protected in the country. WWF provided support necessary to Defensores de la Naturaleza (Defenders of Nature), a Guatemalan nongovernmental organization long interested in the area, to complete an initial technical and feasibility study of Sierra de las Minas for its legal establishment as a protected area by the Guatemalan Congress. This study was completed and taken to the National Congress. The designation as Biosphere Reserve was awarded in October of 1990, ending the first chapter of this effort.

Overall management authority for the Biosphere Reserve has now been delegated to Defensores de la Naturaleza, in recognition of their leading role in the reserve's establishment. A governing commission has been set up to oversee the managers. The planned management program for the reserve has several components: wildland protection and management; environmental education; applied scientific research; and promotion of environmentally sound development with area communities.

Various organizations in addition to Defensores, including WWF, The Nature Conservancy (TNC), CARE, the World Parks Endowment, Conservation International and the Swedish Children's Rain

Forest Fund are providing assistance to different components of the project.

The Project

The overall project effort at the Sierra is quite ambitious. The goals of the Sierra de las Minas management program are to: protect biodiversity and the forests of the Sierra; maintain and improve the watershed function of the Sierra; improve the quality of life of local residents in accordance with sustainable utilization of the natural resources in the area; and promote scientific research in the area.

WWF is currently providing technical and financial support to Defensores to develop and manage both a long-term community development project and an environmental education program in the buffer zone of the newly created Sierra de las Minas Biosphere Reserve. These projects aim to promote a new relationship between people and their environment through introduction of alternative resource use practices and new information, while teaching the means to adapt and expand these in accord with the local reality.

The community development project is composed of permanent, on-site extension work in sustainable agricultural techniques with Kekchi residents in the northern zone of the reserve, on the slopes above the Polochic River valley. Technically, the project is working with a few simple soil conservation techniques: in-row, alternative planting distances, elimination of burning as an agricultural practice, incorporation of organic matter into the tilled areas, the use of green manures (leguminous cover crops that convert atmospheric nitrogen into a form retrievable in the soil), and contour ditches for water management.

These practices are all fairly simple and immediately applicable within the socioeconomic means of the Kekchi farmers. When applied properly, they result in an appreciable increase in production. This is already visible in some of the participants' plots. Once the fundamental base of basic food production is assured, it appears that agro-forestry/cash crops (perhaps coffee) will be the most logical next step for the extension program.

In addition to direct extension with farmers, the project also has developed demonstration plots in two strategic areas. It has identified and begun to work with Kekchi farmers in the area, who have shown great interest in the program, training them as community promoters. These people, and others like them, will be crucial to expansion of the program.

Work on the south side of the Sierra has been initiated. This year's plan is to complete a detailed analysis of this section in order to design project activities for the ensuing years. The analysis has focused on industries operating in the area, and their degree of impact/dependence on resources from the Sierra. The eight municipalities in the southern zone are being studied to determine their level and type of dependency on the natural resource base for agriculture, industry, domestic use, energy generation, etc. A survey of all the smaller communities along the length of the Sierra will be conducted, followed by an in-depth study of three or four communities that the project selects to initiate work in 1992. The program on the south side in year two will strive to address both the industrial and agricultural pressures.

Next, ongoing extension work will expand into different productive sectors, and into the remaining two of three geographically-distinct zones in the reserve. Environmental education will continue for local authorities, and will also be incorporated into the extension activities. All of these activities will be coordinated closely with the research, protection and natural resource management programs.

Lessons Learned:

- *Start where people are located, focus the project on what they already do.*
- *Identify major environmental and economic problems and their nexus, and look for alternative methods, techniques, and organizational structures to address these problems.*
- *Design simple and limited project interventions to begin to share these alternatives with interested people.*
- *Induce experimentation on a small scale with these new ideas.*
- *Adapt and perfect the new approaches, in partnership with the interested local participants.*
- *Extend them horizontally (geographically) through the incorporation of successful participants as local promoters.*
- *Increase the range of activities of the project as the community gains confidence and becomes more innovative.*

BIODIVERSITY ON THE ALTIPLANO
A Case Study on Bolivian Greenhouses

Randall L. Hoag
Food for the Hungry

FOOD FOR THE HUNGRY is an organization of Christian motivation, committed to working with poor people to overcome hunger and poverty through relief and integrated self-development. Founded in 1971, Food for the Hungry is incorporated in both the United States and Switzerland and works in fifteen countries of Asia, Africa, and Latin America.

Food for the Hungry/Bolivia (FH/B) began operations in 1978 and now concentrates its work regions in the rural "altiplano" departments of La Paz, Oruro, and Potosi. The altiplano is a region of high plains ranging from twelve thousand to fourteen thousand feet. It is generally arid and cold with seasonal rains occurring during December through March. Natural resources include tin, silver, gold, high-altitude grains, potatoes, and wool products.

Due to the harsh conditions, very little can grow naturally in the altiplano. Potatoes and grains are the staple foods for rural peasants, with little intake of proteins and vegetables. The only available vegetables are purchased in the city or from truckers by the higher-income peasants. United Nations Children's Fund (UNICEF) determined that Bolivia's altiplano peasants receive an average of 1,804 calories per day against a standard minimum of 2,600. For these reasons and others, Bolivia's infant mortality is 108 out of 1000 before the age of one, one of the highest in the western hemisphere.

Greenhouses

In response to these needs, FH/B began testing greenhouses in the altiplano. After several years of trial and error, FH/B began significant replication of family level greenhouses in 1988, with over one thousand constructed since. In addition, there is evidence of increasing spontaneous replications. The key funder has been the United States Agency for International Development (USAID) via Title II grain monetization.

The majority of the greenhouses are 3 x 10 meters, with adobe walls and Bolivian-made plastic over the top. The cost is under $100. After a course in construction, the families build the adobe structure, windows and ventilators. FH/B makes a onetime donation of plastic and roof ribbing and provides ongoing training. A condition for building a greenhouse is close access to water. A fully producing greenhouse needs 68 liters of water per day. This condition is often met with family level wells that FH/B also helps families build.

In regions where nothing but potatoes and grains would normally grow, rural peasants now enjoy a biodiversity of tomatoes, lettuce, cucumbers, spinach, carrots, and almost any vegetable that they try. Even corn, watermelons, and more exotic plants are being grown. Production levels have reached and surpassed standard levels for international production.

The plastic, which is the most vulnerable part of the greenhouse, has lasted four years and is holding up with proper maintenance. The plastic is specially treated for ultra-violet rays, is 0.025 cm in thickness, and results in an average annual high of 25.5 degrees Celsius and an average low of 3 degrees Celsius.

Lessons Learned

- *Do fewer projects and do them well. FH/B previously did many project types, creating difficulties in quality control, information, and supervision.*
- *Carefully choose a specialty so that it responds to a general felt need, and investigate the experience of other organizations.*
- *The sustainability of family level projects is key. Community level greenhouses tended to be abandoned since no one felt ownership.*
- *Close access to water is needed.*
- *Demonstration greenhouses should be complemented by extension work. Demonstration centers and greenhouses alone did not result in replications.*
- *Training, both in groups and individually, is important. Due to differences in understanding and ability, peasants have not accomplished uniform levels of production.*

- *Poor people value quick results. Peasants see the fruit of their labors on greenhouses within one month. Many have been moved to tears.*
- *Use local and Bolivian-made products for long-range sustainability. Efforts are now being made to create a direct link between plastic manufacturers and community organizations.*
- *Decentralize planning, monitoring, and evaluation for motivation, and standardize designs for quality control.*
- *Leave room for creativity in the standard designs. Peasants have found cost-saving innovations and new plant types.*

Environmental Implications

The family level greenhouses address environmental concern for providing (if not conserving preexisting) biodiversity. At the same time they are neutral in their impact on the environment. Since they effectively create a microenvironment with the primary resource being sunshine, they appear neither to add to nor drain preexisting natural sources. Ultimately, environmental neutrality is positive, as almost any foreign impact has the potential to destabilize it in the long run. There are many examples of this, including the introduction of sheep to Bolivia by the Spaniards three hundred years ago. The sheep's grazing habits, different from indigenous llamas and alpacas, deforested much of the altiplano's natural pastures. Other questions about the environmental implications of the greenhouses follow.

- What could happen to the environment if the greenhouses (or any other project) are a long run success? Water is not currently a problem since the greenhouses are dispersed and use little water. What current peasant customs that affect the environment might be abandoned if greenhouses continue to replicate?
- What about plant disease? At present this does not seem to be a problem since the diseases (normally fungus) are controllable and are isolated in the microenvironment within the greenhouse.

These are the types of questions that continually need to be asked and answered for greenhouses and other development projects. Development workers should take a closer look at environmental neutrality, analyze long-range effects, and ask themselves: what could go wrong if this project is a success?

CASE FOUR

MISSIONARY EARTHKEEPING[1]

Calvin B. DeWitt
Au Sable Institute

WILLIAM CAREY, WIDELY ACKNOWLEDGED AS a principal founder of modern missions, was by today's standards a peculiar missionary. Not only did he understand biblical teachings, he was also an amateur botanist who deeply respected the natural world. As the founder of the Agricultural and Horticultural Society of India, a member of the Linnaean Society, and a conservationist, he understood and practiced missionary earthkeeping. In a paper published in 1811, he made an unprecedented call for forest conservation. But, in the words of a missionary to Pakistan, Dennis Testerman, "Carey's call has gone unheeded by and large; not only in South Asia but around the world, forests have been and continue to be decimated."[2]

While the purpose of Christian missions is a saving one, mission work often results in loss of the sustaining environment of forests, fisheries, and farming. With Amazon botanical explorer, Ghillean T. Prance, we recognize that the environmental impact of missions ranges from good to bad and, however good the intentions, mission work generally does not include adequate consideration or knowledge of environmental factors.[3]

Historically, ecologically harmful mission practice includes conscious forest destruction. Examples abound, from monks in the Middle Ages who appeared "sometimes axe in hand, at the head of a troupe of believers scarcely converted, or of pagans surprised and indignant, to cut down the sacred trees, and thus root out popular superstition,"[4] to an early twentieth century Belgian Congo (Zaire) missionary who is reputed to have said, "I made up my mind that I would make it my work to bring the heathen out of the forest, to give them sunlight, to show them how to live in God's open world, to teach them to abandon this darkness...It was wonderful to see the forest coming down on all sides. I could feel the power of Satan receding as every tree fell."[5]

On the other hand history reveals the ecologically good: the well-known St. Francis of Assisi who modeled humility and respect for Creation; early twentieth century missionary Toyohiko Kagawa who has influenced Japanese land reform and mountain reforestation; and Southern Baptist missionary Luther Copeland who brought people beyond stewardship to being priests of Creation who revere Creation as God's handiwork.[6]

Ours clearly is a time of unprecedented worldwide environmental degradation, including:

1. alteration of Earth's energy exchange with the sun, with consequent acceleration of global warming and destruction of the protective ozone shield;

2. degradation that includes habitat loss, cropland loss, erosion, salinization and desertification;

3. water quality degradation of groundwater, lakes, rivers and oceans;

4. deforestation that annually destroys 100,000 square kilometers of primary forest;

5. species extinction that daily destroys over three species of plants and animals;

6. global toxification that brings DDT to Antarctic penguins and distributes poisons worldwide by wind and currents; and

7. human and cultural degradation of long-standing indigenous peoples and family farms, together with the information contained in plant and animal genes, in ecological relations, and in intergenerational farming experience.[7]

We are led to ask, "Why this degradation?" The biblical answer may be summarized as "arrogance, ignorance, and greed,"[8] or "egocentrism and the selfish nature of people."[9] Unfortunately, the truth of this biblical answer is apparent not only in much of the globalizing monetary market economy but in Christian missions themselves, many of which have helped pave the way for self-interested enterprise and have participated in Creation's degradation. Yet it is to combatting this human problem of arrogance, ignorance, and greed that much of the Bible is addressed. James Gustafson, missionary in Thailand, summarizes these biblical teachings as follows:

if you want to be great, then serve
if you want to be first, be last
if you want to live, die
if you want to be strong, be weak

if you want to be good, admit you're bad
do not curse, but bless
do not take, but give
do not love yourself only, but love your neighbor
　　as you love yourself.

This leads us to ask, "Why do many Christian missions find themselves as complicit participants in Creation's destruction?" Economist Herman E. Daly is helpful in understanding why such well-intended enterprise can go awry—even destroying what it has come to save. He identifies two vitally important questions: "How does the world work?" and "What is right?"[10] To act properly in Creation, those who know the right must also know the principles whereby Earth and its ecosystems maintain their integrity. Those who know the right from the Book must also know the goodness and rightness of Creation as affirmed by the Bible (Gen. 1; Ps. 19:1; Rom. 1:20; Acts 14:17).

But where can we find the answer to the first question, "How does the world work?" The answer is in part in books and courses on ecology and environmental studies in colleges, universities and seminaries. Still more resides in the minds, stories, and practices of local people. Ghillean Prance relates how the Chacobo Indians of Bolivia use nearly every available tree species for medicines, edible fruits, fuel, and craft and building materials; how the Bora Indians of Peru engage in sound ecological practice and agro-forestry; and how the Kayapo Indians of the Amazon have created forest trails that are living, self-restoring "supermarkets."[11] Other examples are a bushman who was able to identify by name two hundred six out of two hundred eleven collected plant varieties and could draw finer distinctions between them than a botanist; the Filipino Hanunoo tribe where adults could identify sixteen hundred different species—some four hundred more than previously recorded in a systematic botanical survey. Often indigenous people are superior to scientists not only in knowledge of species but also in empirically understanding ecosystems.[12] Traditional agricultural technology can also be superior. In the lowland tropics of southeastern Mexico, people managed agroecosystems for centuries to sustain crop yields for the long-term rather than maximizing for the short-term,[13] and in Sri Lanka, forest gardens were created over centuries as analogs—dynamic equivalents—of natural forests by substituting plants useful to people while maintaining forest structure.[14]

Yet such knowledge is rarely recognized or respected by missionaries (or by economic development people), and often is supplanted by practices that replace life-sustaining diversity and life-styles with an agricultural system dependent upon a single crop. Perhaps even more seriously, the goodness of Creation and its God-ordained integrity, affirmed in the Scriptures that the missionaries have come to preach, is neglected.

Does our pointing to the often-superior knowledge of indigenous people mean that they have no need for what missions can give? Ghillean Prance shows why "no" is the answer to this question.

> Anyone who has travelled among the Indians can see the good points...in reference to ecological awareness and at the same time the evil in their lives, often expressed in fighting, raids, poisoning, and like activities. Thus, the effort...is not to portray French philosopher Jean Jacques Rousseau's concept of the "noble savage," for all have sinned and come short of the glory of God.

"How does the world work?" The answer to this question lies in developing a basic knowledge of ecology, and respectful learning from the people who for generations have lived sustainably on the land. Missionary earthkeeping also depends upon answering the question "What is right?" The answer includes Gustafson's summary of the scriptures listed above, and the ecological teachings of the scriptures, including the care and keeping of the earth (Gen. 2:15), the blessing of fruitfulness to nonhuman as well as to human beings (Gen. 1), the preservation of Creation's fruitfulness and regenerative potential (Gen. 6:19–20; Deut. 22:6; 20–19a), provision of sabbath rest for the creatures and Creation (Exod. 23:10–12 and Lev. 25–26), not muddying the waters and trampling the pastures (Ezek. 34:18–19), not covering the land with fields and houses (Isa. 5:8), acknowledging God as Creator and Owner (Neh. 9:6; 1 Chron. 29:11), and being a disciple of the Final Adam through whom the world was created and is reconciled (1 Cor. 15:20–22; Col. 1:15–20; Rom. 5).

For James Gustafson, a present-day missionary earthkeeper with a model mission in Thailand, missionary earthkeeping is work that recognizes that "the true value system of the gospel is constantly at loggerheads with the value systems of all societies."[15] For him it is missionary work that does not seek the "formal correspondence" espoused by much of the worldwide church in its current programs and practice—a correspondence that has brought a "clean" treeless environment and private ownership to a village in Zaire through a mission station described by Mutombo Mpanya;[16] conversion of the Brazilian

Palikur Indians from a hunting-gathering style to a market economy that made them dependent upon the mission and exploitable by others; and transformation of nomads to sedentary life with consequent overuse of local pastures and firewood.[17] For Gustafson, missionary earthkeeping seeks a "dynamic equivalence." This means placing emphasis on the message while using the local ecological situation and local forms and expressions for communicating the message and putting it into practice: "the form changes but the message stays the same."[18]

What is missionary earthkeeping? It is mission work that addresses our two basic questions, honestly acting upon a full understanding *both* of what is right *and* of how the world works. It is enterprise whose mission and goal is wholeness, integrity, and renewal of people, Creator, and Creation and their interrelationships; it is reconciliation of all things (1 Cor. 15:20–22; Col. 1:15–20; Rom. 5). Missionary earthkeeping is not limited by historical models, but is inspired to find new forms, such as Gustafson's integrated holistic development and Robert Clobus' "small gardens as green lights of hope in a land of yellow dryness" in Ghana.[19]

Lessons Learned

- *Two questions must be addressed for any enterprise, including missions: "How does the world work?" and "What is right?"*
- *Neither question is sufficient by itself. If one knows the answer to one, but not the other, trouble lurks.*
- *Knowing how the world works, but not what is right, leads to exploitation and subjugation of the world to selfish ends. Economic enterprises are prone to do this.*
- *Knowing what is right, but not how the world works, leads to violating the principles whereby Creation is ordered, even if intentions are good. Missions are prone to do this.*
- *Every enterprise should honestly act upon a full understanding both of what is right and of how the world works, with economic enterprise paying particular attention to the question of "What is right?" and missions paying particular attention to the question of "How does the world work?"*

Missionary earthkeepers *keep* the Earth in its marvelous integrity, while so serving[20] others that they too can *keep* the Earth. Missionary earthkeepers so behave on Earth that heaven will not be a shock to them.

Notes

1. This paper is based in part upon the book by Ghillean T. Prance and Calvin B. DeWitt, eds., *Missionary Earthkeeping* (Macon, Georgia: Mercer University Press, 1992, in press), a product of the annual Au Sable Forums on Christianity and ecology held at Au Sable Institute of Environmental Studies, 7526 Sunset Trail, N.E., Mancelona, Michigan. Contributors are J. Mark Thomas, Dennis E. Testerman, Robert Clobus, Mutombo Mpanya, and James W. Gustafson.
2. See "Missionary Earthkeeping: Glimpses of the Past, Visions of the Future," in *Missionary Earthkeeping*, eds. Ghillean T. Prance and Calvin B. DeWitt (Macon, Georgia: Mercer University Press, 1992, in press).
3. Prance, "Ecological Awareness," in *Missionary Earthkeeping*, 1992, in press.
4. Quote of Montalembert in his *Monks of the West* as recorded by Testerman, "Missionary Earthkeeping: Past and Future," in *Missionary Earthkeeping*, Ghillean T. Prance and Calvin B. DeWitt, (Macon, Georgia: Mercer University Press, 1992, in press).
5. Testerman, "Missionary Earthkeeping: Past and Future," in *Missionary Earthkeeping*, 1992, in press.
6. Testerman, "Missionary Earthkeeping: Past and Future," in *Missionary Earthkeeping*, 1992, in press.
7. An expanded version of these seven degradations is given in Calvin B. DeWitt, ed., *The Environment and the Christian: What Can We Learn from the New Testament?* (Grand Rapids, Michigan: Wm. B. Eerdmans, 1991).
8. Missionaries themselves are not immune to arrogance, as indicated in the following quote from Gustafson, "Integrated Holistic Development," in *Missionary Earthkeeping*, 1992, in press. He quotes the head of the Thai immigration department in Bangkok as saying, "Missionaries never listen and never try to learn who we are and what we are. They are always trying to tell us something. I feel that missionaries are the most selfish people I know!"
9. This is James Gustafson's redefinition of sin for the cultural setting in which his Thai mission works as described in " Integrated Holistic Development," in *Missionary Earthkeeping*, 1992, in press.
10. Herman E. Daly, "A Biblical Economic Principle and the Steady-State Economy," Au Sable Forum papers. (Mancelona, Michigan: Au Sable Institute, 1986).
11. Prance, "Ecological Awareness," in *Missionary Earthkeeping*, 1992, in press.
12. N. Awa, "Participation and Indigenous Knowledge in Rural Development," *Knowledge* 10 (1989): 304.
13. S. Gliessman, E. Garcia and A. Amador, "The Ecological Basis for the Application of Traditional Agricultural Technology in the Management of Tropical Agro-Ecosystems," *Agro-Ecosystems* 7(1981): 173.
14. J. Moles, "Agricultural Sustainability and Traditional Agriculture: Learning From the Past and Its Relevance to Sri Lanka," *Human Organization* 48 (1989): 70.
15. Gustafson, "Integrated Holistic Development," in *Missionary*

Earthkeeping, 1992, in press.
16. Mutombo Mpanya, "The Impact of PVO Projects: A Zairian Village Case Study," in *Missionary Earthkeeping,* eds. Ghillean T. Prance and Calvin B. DeWitt (Macon, Georgia: Mercer University Press, 1992, in press).
17. Prance, "Ecological Awareness," in *Missionary Earthkeeping,* 1992, in press.
18. Gustafson, "Integrated Holistic Development," in *Missionary Earthkeeping,* 1992, in press.
19. Robert Clobus, "Ecofarming and Land Ownership in Ghana," in *Missionary Earthkeeping,* eds. Ghillean T. Prance and Calvin B. DeWitt (Macon, Georgia: Mercer University Press, 1992, in press).
20. By "serving" here is meant that of the type described in *The Bible* Phil. 2:6–8.

CASE FIVE

FOOD AND FAMINE IN ETHIOPIA
Weapons Against Cultural Diversity

Jason W. Clay
Cultural Survival

*On October 16, 1985, Dr. Jason W. Clay, Director of Research at
Cultural Survival, presented a version of the following case study to
the Subcommittees on Africa and Human Rights of the Committee
on Foreign Affairs in the U.S. House of Representatives.*

IN 1980, AS DIRECTOR OF Research at Cultural Survival, I began to
interview systematically refugees from Ethiopia about the persecution
and discrimination that caused them to flee the country. My intent
was to document the human rights violations that were occurring in
areas of Ethiopia where outsiders were not allowed free access.

Our interviews indicated that the government was attempting to
destroy systematically the culturally distinct groups within the country
by creating a strong central state dominated by the Amhara ethnic
group. Their tactic was to confiscate land, move dissident peoples
from their own areas onto the lands of others and impose, under the
guise of state socialism, local organizations that destroyed the ability
of communities to produce their own food. Ethiopia succeeded in
making communities food aid dependent even though the state could
not provide food for them. While other countries, and even other
groups in Ethiopia, have used food as a weapon, what made this
program particularly loathsome was that hunger and famine were
mere by-products of the government's attempts to destroy specific
cultural groups, or "nation peoples," within the country. This is the
context within which Western humanitarian assistance was being used.

The government's policy to create communities dependent upon
the state exacerbated the 1984–85 famine in northern Ethiopia. As a

result of the government's resettlement policies, famine even spread to the southwest, where rainfall and agricultural production were high in 1984. The government used famine relief to ensure socially and economically dependent populations.

In February and March 1985, a team of three individuals investigated the causes of famine in Ethiopia by interviewing those directly affected: Ethiopian refugees in Sudan. Nearly 250 interviews were conducted privately, away from Sudanese officials or representatives of the various liberation fronts. Interviewees were selected on the basis of a mathematically calculated random sample at each location. This research on the causes of famine was the most scientifically conducted, on the largest sample, by any government or private agency. It challenged assumptions upon which most humanitarian assistance from the West had been based.

To the first question before the subcommittee, "Is the Government of Ethiopia engaging in a policy of deliberate starvation of its own people, particularly in dissident regions of the country?" the answer is complicated, but unequivocally "yes." Government policies have destroyed food supplies, disrupted normal commerce that would have allowed individuals to acquire food, prevented people from reaching food, withheld food from those in need, forcibly relocated people well away from their own ample food supplies, and imposed crushing tax and contribution levels on peasant producers, which forced them to sell their food and productive assets such as oxen or even seed.

The government centralized state authority to an extent that was not projected even under previous Amhara-dominated governments. Peasant producers in the southwest, for example, insisted that they paid more to the current Amhara-dominated central government than they ever did to landlords and tax collectors in the past.

The following four samples demonstrate how government policies varied from area to area.

The Contested Areas of Tigray

- People from contested Tigrayan Peoples' Liberation Front (TPLF) areas could not safely go to government feeding centers and receive food without being resettled.
- People indicated that they were denied food at government feeding centers because they did not have the required identification.
- Seventy-seven percent of the famine victims interviewed

indicated that from 1982-84 the army burned houses in their villages as well as crops in the field, piled for threshing or stored in granaries or houses.

- Twenty-five percent of those interviewed indicated that, within the past three years, the army had stolen their oxen, their farm equipment and food.
- Everyone from the contested areas indicated that the army attacked during periods of planting and harvesting to reduce agricultural production and make the areas more dependent on the state. Delays in planting did not allow farmers to take advantage of early rains, a critical factor when rains ended early in 1983 and 1984. Delays in planting also allowed both weeds (striga) and insects (armyworms) to become established in fields before crops even sprouted. Some 90 percent reported that army worms were the major cause of famine. According to experts in the United States, the parasitic weed striga, which attacks the roots of crops, can cause losses of up to 90 percent.

Government Held Areas of Wollo and Tigray

- Peasant associations were required to "nominate" their quota for resettlement before residents were given food. For example, 75 percent of those interviewed from Wollo indicated that their peasant association sent them to government centers to get food rations. Instead, they were arrested and resettled.
- Those "nominated" for resettlement often included young men who were thought to be potential TPLF recruits, under government suspicion, or out of favor with local officials. Moslem areas of Wollo also appeared to have had more people taken for resettlement.
- Many from Wollo indicated that production from their land can be high but erratic; many years it yields very little. In the past, farmers had saved grain from the good years to tide them over when production was poor. Government policies that mandated the appropriation of surpluses each year created famine during the lean years.

The Resettlement Program

- The death rates reported for the resettlement sites ranged from 33 to 270 per 10,000 per day.
- Contrary to government reports, none of those we interviewed resettled voluntarily. They were guarded throughout the move as well as in the new sites. Ten percent reported seeing people who tried to escape killed.
- Eighty-six percent said they had been forcibly separated from some or all of their family.
- Twenty percent of the people taken from the same villages died before they arrived at the resettlement camps. Relatives who brought food to those in holding camps before the trip to the Southwest were denied entry and beaten.
- Sixty percent of those resettled from Tigray reported that they had been imprisoned during the resettlement process.
- Sixty percent of those interviewed reported that they saw people die en route to the resettlement sites.
- Those resettled were given one or two pieces of bread per day and very little water. The lack of food, people guessed, was to weaken them so they would not attempt to escape.
- Forty percent of those resettled from Tigray and Wollo reported that they had been beaten either during resettlement or at the sites.

People Displaced in Southwestern Ethiopia

- Half of those who fled from Ethiopia to Yabuus, Sudan, indicated that the government had taken their land. Although this land was seized for resettlement, most was not used.
- Seventy-five percent of those interviewed in Yabuus indicated that required attendance at village meetings during key periods of agricultural labor significantly reduced production.
- Sixty-three percent said that the disarming of the local population left them defenseless to protect their crops from wild animals.
- Forty percent of those in Yabuus reported that high taxes and "voluntary" contributions forced farmers to sell oxen or even seed and thus reduced their productivity.
- More than one-third reported that the four-to-five days per

week of forced, unpaid labor required on communal peasant association plots during key periods left them little time to work on their own plots.

- More than eighty-six percent of those interviewed indicated that their imprisonment for such crimes as missing meetings, not paying taxes, fees or contributions, refusing to arrest a friend or neighbor, speaking up at meetings, questioning the local officials' decisions, or being Oromo kept them from their fields. If an individual missed a peasant association meeting he was punished with ten days in prison. Imprisonment during the planting or weeding periods greatly reduced total production.

In the future, in Ethiopia and similar countries, foreign donors (especially Americans) must seriously consider the kinds of conditions they want to perpetuate through famine or development assistance programs sponsored either by their governments or government funded NGOs.

Lessons Learned

The following precautions would help Western agencies avoid letting countries like Ethiopia use their food for less than humanitarian purposes.

- *Find out why there is famine. Examine the causes. Interview those who are starving in addition to government officials, academics, and other so-called experts. Undertake this research systematically so that it can be replicated and compared with that of other researchers or agencies.*
- *Always ask, "Will this assistance eradicate or exacerbate the conditions that led to the present famine?"*
- *Do not delay efforts to feed those who are starving but make sure that the systems that are being set up can be modified as answers to the first two points are gathered.*
- *Avoid working through states, particularly when nation peoples are the famine victims.*
- *Feed people at home, do not ask them to move or take part in programs that force them to move.*
- *Apply all restrictions, monitoring systems and research requirements equally to both sides.*

Minimally, make sure that the help does not hurt.

Bibliography

Clay, Jason, and Bonnie Halcomb. *Politics and the Ethiopian Famine, 1984–1985.* Cultural Survival Report 20 (Cambridge, Mass.: Cultural Survival, 1985).

"Food and Famine in Ethiopia—Weapons Against Cultural Diversity." *Cultural Survival Quarterly* 9 no. 4 (1985): 47–50.

"Ethiopia Refugees Flee Collectivization." *Cultural Survival Quarterly* 10 no. 2 (1986): 60–65. Reprinted in *Pogrom.*

Clay, Jason, Sandra Steingrabera, and Peter Niggli. *The Spoils of Famine: Ethiopian Famine Policy and Peasant Agriculture.* Cultural Survival Report 25 (Cambridge, Mass.: Cultural Survival, 1988).

"Ethiopian Famine and Relief Agencies." In *The Moral Nation: Humanitarian and U. S. Foreign Policy Today,* edited by B. Nichols and G. Loescher, 232–277. Notre Dame: University of Notre Dame Press, 1989.

GETTING TO GATT

Eric Thor and Neilson C. Conklin
Arizona State University
Center for Agribusiness Policy Studies

A NEWCOMER TO AGRICULTURAL POLICY may feel as though she or he has passed through a looking glass into a topsy-turvy world where policies are backward. Developed nations tax consumers to subsidize small numbers of relatively wealthy farmers, while many developing nations exploit impoverished farmers to subsidize wealthier urban consumers! The dumping of surplus production on world markets by developed countries has depressed agricultural prices but it has not eliminated hunger. It has also discouraged the development of ecologically and economically sustainable agriculture in developing nations.

Although some national policies may seem rational when viewed in isolation, their combined effect has been to discourage food production where it is most needed. Additionally, in developed countries, world food policies encourage intensive farming in environmentally fragile areas and increase volatility in world markets. Taken globally, existing agricultural policies are not only economically inefficient but they:

- are regressive, transferring wealth from the poor to the rich;
- reduce food security[1]; and
- contribute to the development of environmentally unsustainable agricultural systems.

The reform of these upside-down policies was a major reason for the Uruguay Round of multilateral trade negotiations under the General Agreement on Tariffs and Trade (GATT) that began in 1986. Fundamental policy reform raised the prospect of more stable agricultural markets, the elimination of artificial incentives for intensive farming in fragile environments, and increased incentives for food production in many developing nations. Today, as we near the end of this effort, the outcome remains uncertain.

A Brief History of GATT

In the first round of GATT in 1948, twenty-three nations agreed to negotiate a new set of international trade rules, the General Agreement on Tariffs and Trade. Then, memories of "beggar thy neighbor" trade policies were still fresh. These policies had plunged economies around the world into the "great depression." GATT was an attempt by industrialized nations to avoid such an economic catastrophe in the post-World War II world. Today, as in 1948, GATT consists of three basic rules:

1. *Most-favored-nation treatment* requires that national policies affecting trade apply equally to all GATT members;
2. *National treatment* requires that policies affecting domestic commerce may not discriminate against imports; and
3. *Prohibition of nontariff barriers* means that tariffs are the only sanctioned trade policies for GATT members.

A small, truly multinational staff at the GATT Secretariat in Geneva administers the rules and facilitates multilateral negotiations. GATT was responsible for much of the increase in global trade and economic growth in the three decades following World War II. This success hinged on the shift from nontariff policies, like quotas, to tariffs. Tariffs were followed by multilateral tariff reductions. Trade liberalization began with a "round" of negotiations in 1947 at Annecy, France. Later rounds, including the Dillon Round (1960–62), the Kennedy Round (1963–67), and the Tokyo Round (1973–79), led to further reductions in trade barriers. Agriculture was not part of these discussions.

Agriculture and GATT Today on the Road to Policy Reform

In the past, agriculture was left behind in negotiations because broad exceptions to rules on nontariff barriers were negotiated at GATT's inception. These exceptions, including the "Section 22 waiver,"[2] which allows the United States to impose nontariff barriers for many agricultural commodities, led to increasing restrictions on agricultural trade. Worldwide, nominal protection rates for agricultural products rose from 21 percent in 1965 to 28 percent in 1974, and soared to 40 percent by 1988. This dramatically increased the cost of federal programs. This lack of discipline on trade policies has been partly responsible for the topsy-turvy nature of agricultural policies around the world.

The inherent contradictions in existing agricultural policies became increasingly apparent in the 1980s. As prices tumbled, farmers around the world struggled. The farm subsidies cost rose in developed nations. By 1986, when the Uruguay Round of negotiations began at Punte Del Este, Uruguay, the annual budgetary cost of farm subsidies in both the United States and the European Community (EC) exceeded $30 billion a year. The high cost of agricultural policies and their failure to solve problems of farmers and consumers around the world led GATT members to place global agricultural policy reform at the top of the negotiating agenda. But nearly two years after its scheduled conclusion, the Uruguay Round, made up of 176 negotiating nations, is stuck, mired in the debate over agricultural policy reform. All nations seem unwilling to look at global, rather than national or regional, policy consequences. These same political-economic forces led to today's topsy-turvy policies that have stalled the negotiations.

Unable to Negotiate a Solution?

The United States opened negotiations with a proposal to eliminate all "trade distorting" subsidies over ten years. This was followed by a similar proposal from the "Cairns Group"[3] of "non-subsidizing exporters" led by Australia. The United States and the Cairns Group viewed multilateral reform as a way to increase global economic welfare, stabilize agricultural markets, and replace farmers' dependence on government with income from export markets. These proposals met with stiff resistance from both the EC and Japan, which have the heaviest subsidies and strong farm lobbies. Additionally, Congress must approve whatever the president and the trade representative seek in negotiations. The United States has since modified its proposal, which is currently based on four concepts:

1. *Market access* would convert all nontariff barriers to tariffs. Then it is hoped that all nations could reduce them over time;

2. *Export competition* would phase out export subsidies and prohibit export embargoes (bona fide food aid programs would be allowed);
3. *Internal support* would require "substantial progressive reduction" of the most trade distorting domestic policies (for example, U.S. income supports and EC price intervention); and
4. *Sanitary and phytosanitary regulations* would establish a process for resolving trade disputes involving human, plant, and animal health issues on the basis of scientific evidence.

Today, the U.S. proposal also recognizes the unique problems facing developing nations and offers them special consideration in implementing the import access and internal support parts of the proposal.

The impasse among nations at GATT results primarily from the United States' unwillingness to compromise further and the EC's unwillingness to accept the U.S. proposal. Resistance by the EC revolves around market access and export competition. Unlike U.S. agricultural policy, which is based on government payments to farmers, the EC's Common Agricultural Policy (CAP) subsidizes farmers through price guarantees. Thus U.S. taxpayers pay most subsidy costs while consumers bear most of the burden in Europe.

The CAP is based on three principles: common pricing, community preference (EC products are preferred over imports), and EC financing. The primary tools for implementing the CAP are minimum price levels supported by import restrictions using a variable levy (an import tax that rises as world prices fall), and export restitutions (subsidies), needed to set high-priced surpluses on depressed world markets. Measured in terms of output, the CAP has been very successful; a net grain importer fifteen years ago, the EC today is a substantial grain exporter. However, this self-sufficiency has come at the cost of high food prices for European consumers and lost markets for developed and developing country exporters.

Loss of the variable levy and export restitutions under the U.S. proposal would force the EC to significantly reduce support to farmers or to use less distorting policies supported by taxpayers rather than consumers. Some EC governments are willing to accept the political costs of reducing farm supports but not the costs of higher taxes. Others are unwilling to accept reduced supports at any price. Thus the EC finds itself unable to accept fundamental reform of agricul–tural policy without upsetting the Community's internal political balance. Recent demonstrations by French farmers illustrate the political problems GATT raises for the EC. The emergence of Eastern European nations as competitors in European markets[4] puts further pressure on EC members, who would like to assist Eastern European development through trade but cannot afford the domestic political costs of increased agricultural imports.

Back on the Road to Reform?

The possibility of a compromise on agricultural trade at GATT remains, primarily because GATT members do not want to give up the gains they have made in other areas during the Uruguay Round. But it seems increasingly unlikely that this GATT round will lead to fundamental changes in agricultural policies. Topsy-turvy policies will likely be with us and they will continue to distort trade, reduce food security, and tax the environment. As faith in GATT's multilateral approach to trade liberalization declines, nations seem to be turning increasingly to the formation of trading blocks, such as the proposed North American Free Trade Agreement linking the United States, Canada, and Mexico. These agreements may help to harmonize policies within trading blocks but they are unlikely to yield the kind of global reform prerequisite for improvements in global food security and the development of more sustainable agricultural systems.

What can we do? Agricultural policy reform cannot be accomplished overnight: it is a long-term goal requiring sustained effort. Topsy-turvy policies cannot be righted without political support. Although interest groups who gain from the current state of affairs are well organized, those who stand to gain from reforms, including consumers and farmers in the developing world, are not well organized and have little political influence. Many other potential supporters of policy reform are simply unaware of the problems agricultural policies are creating for the world. Awareness of the agricultural policy problem is a first step toward generating the political support that a meaningful reform requires. Thus the most important task in getting back on the road toward more sensible policies is education. Your challenge is to learn more about the complicated effects of agricultural policies around the world, to educate others about these policies, and above all question simplistic solutions to the difficult problems of food security and environmental sustainability.

Notes

1. For the purposes of this paper, food security is defined as a physical and economic situation where consumers are ensured an adequate diet. This global concept of food security is distinct from narrow concepts based on a nation's ability to feed its own population.
2. Section 22, a section of the Agricultural Adjustment Act of 1933 (P.L. 73-10) allows the president to restrict imports through the use of quotas and fees if imports threaten to interfere with the operation of Federal price support programs.
3. The Cairns Group formed in 1986 at Cairns, Australia. Members include: Argentina, Australia, Brazil, Canada, Chile, Columbia, Hungary, Indonesia, Malaysia, New Zealand, the Philippines, Thailand, and Uruguay.
4. It is no coincidence that Hungary is a member of the Cairns Group.

Suggested Reading

"Saving Trade," The Economist (Sept. 7, 1991): 17–18.

Krissoff, Barry, John Sullivan, John Wainio, and Brian Johnston. Agricultural Trade Liberalization and Developing Countries. USDA: Economic Research Service, 1990. Staff Report AGES 9042.

Lipton, Katherine L. Agriculture, Trade and the GATT: A Glossary of Terms. USDA: Economic Research Service, 1991. Agr. Inf. Bul. 625.

Olson, Mancur. "Agricultural Exploitation and Subsidization: There is an Explanation." Choices, 5 (4th Quarter 1990): 8–11.

USDA. The GATT Negotiations. USDA: Office of the Press Secretary, 1990a.

USDA. Multilateral Trade Reform: What the GATT Negotiations Mean to U.S. Agriculture. Economic Research Service, 1990b. Staff Briefing.

Appendix II

RESOLUTIONS

ONE

RESOLUTIONS FOR EARTH CHARTER AND AGENDA 21

I. PROTECTION AND MANAGEMENT OF LAND RESOURCES:
   COMBATTING DESERTIFICATION

II. PROTECTION AND MANAGEMENT OF LAND RESOURCES:
    COMBATTING DEFORESTATION

III. PROTECTION AND MANAGEMENT OF LAND RESOURCES:
     STRENGTHENING BIODIVERSITY

IV. HUMAN RIGHTS BASIS FOR ENVIRONMENTALLY SOUND DEVELOPMENT

V. ECONOMIC INSTRUMENTS NEEDED FOR ENVIRONMENTALLY
   SOUND DEVELOPMENT

VI. ETHICAL DIMENSIONS OF ENVIRONMENTALLY SOUND DEVELOPMENT

THESE RESOLUTIONS ARE PRODUCTS OF "Growing Our Future," November 21–22, 1991, a symposium on Food Security and the Environment held in Tempe, Arizona prior to the United Nations Conference on Environment and Development (UNCED). They are put forth for incorporation in Agenda 21, an action agenda for governments for sustainable development in the 21st century, and the Earth Charter, a global charter of rights for the Earth and its inhabitants. The symposium incorporated views from representatives of governmental agencies, universities, private business, conservation groups, social action nonprofits, and churches.

Resolutions were made by consensus in subject-specific drafting groups. No attempt was made to reach consensus by the symposium as a whole, and not every participant agreed with all resolutions made by each drafting group.

I.   PROTECTION AND MANAGEMENT OF LAND RESOURCES: COMBATTING DESERTIFICATION

Be it resolved that:

Agenda 21

1. any natural resource management strategy for a given region must take into account the household food security of the population in the area. Trade-offs may be necessary in policy formulation.
2. the people NGOs work with in areas threatened by desertification should be considered partners rather than beneficiaries in the development process. Their needs will help determine the objectives that are pursued and help identify the indicators that are important for monitoring (NGOs).
3. NGOs should take a more proactive role in identifying vulnerable regions for providing assistance prior to the outbreak of famines. This would include developing the response capability in the vulnerable area, as well as setting up monitoring systems based on coping strategies used by the local population.
4. population growth is a major reason for many of the problems associated with environmental degradation. We must address this problem head on through education and family planning programs (local and national governments).
5. energy use is an important aspect of overexploration of resources. We must focus on energy efficient species and technologies (for example, solar energy) to cut down on the destruction of forests (NGOs).
6. any reforestation or agro-forestry program should take into account the trees, shrubs, and other plants that have indigenous value to the local population. Women especially should play a role in identifying these plants (NGOs).
7. farmers themselves represent an underutilized pool of knowledge for creative interventions. NGOs should strive to identify these ideas for dissemination to other farm families whenever possible.
8. networking will be important for creating a forum for common goals and to avoid duplication. This networking can be promoted through computers, faxes, and meetings. Through such communication, experiences can be shared across nations for combatting desertification.

9. food aid should be made more effective by integrating short-term food security goals with long-term natural resources enhancing interventions. To do this effectively, NGOs must depoliticize food aid from other state agendas.
10. more effort should be made to promote inter- and intraregional transfer of food rather than the promotion of external supplies of food aid (NGOs).
11. land tenure questions will always be intimately linked to natural resource conservation. Land tenure issues must be addressed in a location specific way and not always uniformly. Whenever possible NGOs should support effective community natural resource management activities.
12. "Imagination is more important than knowledge." (Einstein) We need more creative ways to deal with water conservation, food preservation, and livestock management. An important place for NGOs to start is by looking at local indigenous knowledge.

II. PROTECTION AND MANAGEMENT OF LAND RESOURCES: COMBATTING DEFORESTATION

Be it resolved that any resolution regarding land management as it affects deforestation must provide for the following:

Agenda 21

1. addressing and resolving land tenure issues in tropical forest countries.
2. linking the equity and distribution/development issues of indigenous and needy people with the environment/cultural conservation agenda of the world.
3. transferring appropriate technology via local extension systems, where possible, and interceding before desperation sets in.

III. PROTECTION AND MANAGEMENT OF LAND RESOURCES:
STRENGTHENING BIODIVERSITY

Be it resolved that:

Agenda 21

1. development and environment NGOs should work in concert.

Earth Charter

1. development should not detract from, but contribute to, biodiversity through the consideration and evaluation of its effect on the diversity of indigenous environmental, cultural, social and technical systems.

IV. HUMAN RIGHTS BASIS FOR ENVIRONMENTALLY SOUND DEVELOPMENT

Be it resolved that:

Agenda 21

1. the development community should encourage, through its financial support and technical assistance, partnerships among host governments, local NGOs, and interested international agencies.
2. the World Bank, USAID, and UN agencies must report on situations of indigenous people groups in any country to which they provide funds.
3. issues of biodiversity and land conservation should be linked to issues of cultural diversity, poverty, and hunger, and vice versa.

Earth Charter

1. human rights are a necessary prerequisite for sustainable development. Human rights will promote local resource rights. These resource rights will accordingly motivate the protection of resources. In as much as resource rights are inextricably linked to human rights, the economic, social, and environmental costs of any development action must be assessed in terms of opportunities lost or gained by local people upon whose land the actions

occur. These costs must by taken into account by all bilateral and multilateral donors.

V. ECONOMIC INSTRUMENTS NEEDED FOR ENVIRONMENTALLY
    SOUND DEVELOPMENT

Be it resolved that:

Agenda 21

A. International Trade
  1. international trade, environmental protection, the alleviation of hunger and economic development are intrinsically linked and cannot be dealt with in isolation. Rather, an integrated approach to policy development is required that recognizes the potential impacts that changes in one area are likely to have on these other areas of critical concern.
  2. it is imperative that we find ways to halt the further degradation of our global environment and loss of biodiversity, including traditional knowledge of the earth and its species, by shifting to long-term, sustainable systems of production, land use and land tenure.
  3. population growth, illegal drug production and military related environmental degradation are powerful threats to sustainable development and environmental protection, and must be confronted and brought under control by national governments and multinational institutions.
  4. the outcome of GATT negotiations will have impacts worldwide on economic development, food production and the environment—particularly in developing nations. GATT policy decisions must take into account these broader, global impacts rather than just the narrow interests of national industries seeking protection and public subsidies.
  5. the GATT process in the United States and other participating nations should be reformed to provide an opportunity for consumer, environmental and other interested groups to influence policy.

B. Military Research and Spending
  6. government funding for military research and development should be redirected into research and development funding for

new, comprehensive approaches to achieving sustainable economic development along with environmental protection. Specific areas requiring research and development include:

    a. development of early warning and rapid response systems for anticipating and preventing regional food security crises.

    b. development of better models and paradigms for the cost-benefit analysis of economic development and environmental protection alternatives that recognize and take into account nonmonetized costs, such as environmental pollution and degradation, loss of biodiversity, and socioeconomic impacts on traditional cultures and subsistence systems.

    c. development of common, internationally recognized and accepted standards for environmental quality and food safety.

C. Financial Resources

    7. adequate funding must be made available to finance environmentally sustainable economic development. Such funding should include:

    a. agricultural credit to small and medium sized farms to make possible the purchase of inputs needed for sustainable agriculture.

    b. seed capital and business incubation programs to finance and assist innovative new businesses that are environmentally friendly and create employment and income in regions experiencing environmental degradation.

    c. greater priority on assistance to small and medium sized business ventures as opposed to large scale economic development projects that often severely impact the environment.

VI. Ethical Dimensions of Environmentally Sound Development

Be it resolved that:

Agenda 21

A. Technology

    1. efforts be made to develop low-cost, practical sources of energy that are accessible to the poor and minimize negative impact on the environment.

    2. it be recognized that, although it provides useful tools for environmental preservation, technology cannot provide solutions

without the inclusion of underlying social science and ethical considerations.

B. Hunger
   3. the world community has a moral obligation to provide more equitable distribution of the resources that provide nutritionally balanced food to mankind.
   4. governments participating in the GATT process, particularly the U.S. Government, should redirect their GATT negotiators to progressively reduce import tariffs on agricultural products in ways that:
      a. increase food security, providing incentives for agricultural producers in countries experiencing widespread hunger, poverty and food shortages;
      b. anticipate and minimize adverse impacts on the environment, food safety and food producers in countries where food security is a problem;
      c. link tariff reductions with the elimination of price ceilings on food products in developing countries that discourage farmers from producing food crops for domestic consumption;
      d. develop an international, standardized statistical reporting system so that international trade and development can be better monitored and analyzed.

C. Education
   5. we advocate education for responsible earth nurture and management. This education should be promoted from the earliest years, making use of multiple techniques. The goal of such education is household and national food security in relation to environmental integrity.
   6. education efforts should include:
      a. community needs are greater than individual desires and are of individual responsibility to protect and enhance;
      b. the importance of replenishing and restoring land and other resources used;
      c. the contextual development of new educational strategies and innovative thinking to deal with such issues as population pressure and land use;
      d. the immediate establishment of models for study and wider social implementation.

Two

RESOLUTIONS FOR EARTH SUMMIT PARALLEL CONFERENCE ON RELIGION AND ECOLOGY

I. ETHICS AND VALUES IMPLICIT IN ENVIRONMENTALLY SOUND DEVELOPMENT

II. RESOLUTIONS FOR THE CHRISTIAN COMMUNITY

THESE RESOLUTIONS ARE PRODUCTS OF "Growing Our Future," November 21–22, 1991, a symposium on Food Security and the Environment, held in Tempe, Arizona, to prepare for UNCED. The symposium incorporated views from representatives of governmental agencies, universities, private business, conservation groups, social action nonprofits, and churches. No attempt was made to reach consensus by the symposium as a whole. The following views were drafted by representatives of church-based organizations that participated in the symposium:

I. ETHICS AND VALUES IMPLICIT IN ENVIRONMENTALLY SOUND DEVELOPMENT

Be it resolved that:

Earth Charter

1. the UNCED declare the integrity of Creation as its highest priority and make provision and opportunity for each of its member nations to do the same.
2. the goal of integrity of Creation in all its richness and fullness include:
   a. the mutual integrity of people, human society and the biosphere;

b. justice and peace throughout Creation.

3. that a strategy be formulated to meet the goal of Creation's integrity, including:

   a. the halting of Creation's degradation in its many aspects;

   b. restoring Creation's integrity where degraded;

   c. the qualitative and quantitative development of this integrity in societies that have not yet reached material maturity;

   d. encouraging and enabling each person to engage in the care and keeping of some part of Creation.

4. that all institutions—economic, governmental, juridical, charitable, ecclesiastical, educational, and others—be enabled and encouraged to develop the means for making the goal of Creation's integrity their highest priority.

5. that the well-being of people be upheld as the highest priority while at the same time acknowledging importance of the well-being of the entire biosphere.

6. that each family should have the right to enjoy the fruits of Creation and should exercise the responsibility to teach future generations the obligation of stewardship of Creation.

7. that the management of global change, vis-à-vis developmental and environmental sustainability, must acknowledge the symbiotic nature of the principles of ethics and ecosystems. This will include equity, and participation, with particular attention to the needs and rights of those presently marginalized—women, the poor, landless tribal peoples, etc.

8. that development strategies promoted by the countries of the North recognize that technologies appropriate for Creation-centered sustainable development should meet the following criteria:

   a. they should enrich and build upon existing skills and technologies;

   b. they should address the expressed needs of the beneficiary communities through direct participation;

   c. they should be locally made, maintained and operated;

   d. they should enhance environmental and social organisms and systems.

II. Resolutions for the Christian Community

Be it resolved that the Christian community and organizations must:

1. repent, where necessary, of past poor earthkeeping practices.

2. unite with the worldwide Christian church in learning better earthkeeping practices.
3. affirm the proclamation of the Lordship of Jesus Christ over all Creation, and actively include good earthkeeping as a practice taught in Scripture.
4. utilize Christian values as a guide in development, emphasizing human development over technical development.
5. learn from each other practical lessons in good earthkeeping.
6. challenge other religious traditions in better earthkeeping.

INDEX

Other important books from KUMARIAN PRESS:

Breaking the Cycle of Poverty
The BRAC Strategy
CATHERINE H. LOVELL

Democratizing Development
The Role of Voluntary Organizations
JOHN CLARK

Economic Restructuring and African Public Administration
EDITORS: GELASE MUTAHABA, M. JIDE BALOGUN

Enhancing Policy Management Capacity in Africa
EDITORS: GELASE MUTAHABA, M. JIDE BALOGUN

Gender Analysis in Development Planning
A Case Book
EDITORS: ARUNA RAO, MARY B. ANDERSON, CATHERINE A. OVERHOLT

Getting to the 21st Century
Voluntary Action and the Global Agenda
DAVID C. KORTEN

HRD
International Perspectives on Development and Learning
EDITORS: MERRICK JONES, PETE MANN

Improving Family Planning Evaluation
A Step-by-Step Guide for Professionals
JOSÉ GARCÍA-NÚÑEZ

Intermediary NGOs
The Supporting Link in Grassroots Development
THOMAS F. CARROLL

La gestion efficace de projets de developpement
Un guide a l'exécution et l'évaluation
DEUXIEME EDITION
DERICK W. BRINKERHOFF, JANET C. TUTHILL

Management Dimensions of Development
Perspectives and Strategies
MILTON J. ESMAN

Managing Quality of Care in Population Programs
EDITOR: ANRUDH K. JAIN

Opening the Marketplace to Small Enterprise
Where Magic Ends and Development Begins
TON DE WILDE, STIJNTJE SCHREURS, WITH ARLEEN RICHMAN

Promises Not Kept
The Betrayal of Social Change in the Third World
JOHN ISBISTER

Public Administration in Small and Island States
EDITOR: RANDALL BAKER

Toward a Green Central America
Integrating Conservation and Development
EDITORS: VALERIE BARZETTI, YANINA ROVINSKI

Vitalizing African Public Administration
for Recovery and Development
GELASE MUTAHABA, RWEIKIZA BAGUMA, MOHAMED HALFANI
UNITED NATIONS

Working Together
Gender Analysis in Agriculture
EDITORS: HILARY SIMS FELDSTEIN, SUSAN V. POATS

Kumarian Press is dedicated to bringing you quality publications on International Management and Development.

For a complete catalog, please call or write:

Kumarian Press, Inc.
630 Oakwood Avenue, Suite 119
West Hartford, CT 06110-1529 USA

Inquiries 203-953-0214 • Fax 203-953-8579
Toll free (for orders only) 1-800-289-2664